THE SOUTHERN WAY

C000200303

CONTENTS

© Kevin Robertson (Noodle Books) and the various contributors 2013

ISBN 978-1-909328-03-7

First published in 2013 by Kevin Robertson

under the **NOODLE BOOKS** imprint

PO Box 279

Corhampton

SOUTHAMPTON

SO32 3ZX

www.noodlebooks.co.uk

editorial@thesouthernway.co.uk

Printed in England by

Berforts Information Press Ltd.

Publishers note: Every effort has been made to identify and correctly annotate photographic credits. Should an error have occurred then this is entirely unintentional.

Editorial

I regain the editor's chair for this issue, mainly because no one has agreed to pick up the cudgel after the last 'Guest Editorial'. Please, we don't bite, use this page to have your say - a personal 'soapbox' if you like. And that is exactly what I am going to do this time and also the reason for the selection of the image that precede this piece, on pages 2/3.

I start by saying I do not travel by train much nowadays and when I do it, is inevitable that there will be comparisons with what remains compared with what once was. I must be fair and state that the modern railway system bears little in common with the old, traversing the same route perhaps, but apart from that it is almost like a foreign country. I say this because I recently had reason to book a ticket on-line but did not have the faintest idea how to collect it from the automatic ticket machine at the station - 'passenger assistance' - you must be joking. (A young lady came to my rescue.) But once on the train it was in part at least a reasonably pleasant experience. (I have had cause to use three separate rail companies recently, South West Trains, First Great Western, and Cross-Country. I will not list these in order of preference although I cannot avoid one point: why, when loco-hauled trains consisted of perhaps 10 or more coaches on the same service, do modern day operators think that, with what are now increased numbers of 'passengers', we can all fit into a four-coach unit, or am I rather bad at maths?)

So, to return to the theme I had started, turn the page back to the double page spread (the location is Chandlers Ford): what we have is the typical secondary route service of the early BR era, and allowing for a change of motive-power and rolling stock, the type of train that would also have been familiar to generations past.

I have though to admit all this nostalgia comes at a price - literally. Was such a working as seen at Chandlers Ford an economic proposition, and for that matter was all the associated infrastructure of the station here similarly cost-effective? In short, we probably know the answer. For as much as we might care to pretend otherwise the answer has to be a categoric 'no'. How many men (sorry to be sexist at this point but in the 1950s there were few women involved in the operating side of the railway) were involved in running this service - three on board at least. Then there were station staff, signalmen and perhaps slightly less obvious gangers / platelayers, control room staff etc etc. All this for a T9, a 3-car Bulleid set and an odd coach tagged on

the rear. Maybe it was an unbalanced working, maybe on that particular day there was a party of 50 from the Women's Institute which made it profitable - who knows?

The trouble was, that by the 1950s wages had risen whilst receipts had fallen, both passenger and freight. Operating costs most likely exceeded the revenue from this service and yet such trains would continue to be a feature of lines just like these for some years to come.

But at some point there had to be a line drawn. On one side was the 'old' railway as seen here, on the other side would be local dieselisation (at Chandlers Ford it was DEMU sets) but often these were insufficient to retain passengers against a wage and operating cost spiral. Next was Beeching or similar followed by years of under investment in the railway network by successive governments.

It has taken a sea-change, privatisation, to move things forward (and contrary to how it may appear, I voice no opinion whatsoever on the merits of this change). At least now Chandlers Ford still does see a train service, though there was a 30+ year gap when there was nothing - a long time to wait if you had missed the last train back in 1969.

But nowadays that service is not a loco-hauled T9 and Bulleid set, instead garish coloured impersonal diesel units throb east and west at regular intervals. It will take a long time before the operator involved has sufficient confidence to invest in expensive stock with the same degree of service that once existed.

And perhaps that is the nub of my earlier comment about why a 10-coach train is now replaced by a 4-car set; there needs to be confidence that revenue will continue. Is it any different to any of us: why invest in a new car if it is not going to be used?

So as I travel, I will sit back from time to time and imagine how things used to be. Yes, it may be faster today but I still miss the past - hence of course I hope what will be another nostalgia full issue of 'SW' on the following pages.

One final point: I may be a 'customer' but I am also still a 'passenger',. Being dumped unceremoniously (20 miles from my destination late one night due to one operator not talking to another and there being no onward services until the next morning) is not my idea of fun. I seem to recall that once upon a time the passenger came first.

Kevin Robertson

Front cover - No 34029 'Lundy' passing Woolston on the outskirts of Southampton with a heavy Brighton service. For many years these services would detach / attach a portion at Fareham for Portsmouth. Ron Roberts
Rear cover - No 34105 'Swanage' leaving Bournemouth Central with the re-routed 'Pines Express'. Arthur King
Pages 2/3 - Nostalgia at Chandlers Ford. T9 No 30304 leaving the station for Eastleigh with a Salisbury to Portsmouth working. The view is west towards Romsey. Years before, a siding had led off to the left to a brickworks whilst in more recent time Martin Welch has immortalised the location as the fictitious 'Hursley'. Les Elsey
Opposite - Changing times at Waterloo - remember those 'Southern Electric' type covers carrying the platform numbers? The photograph was taken to show what was then new lighting. Waterloo is not like this today. Steve Godden collection

THE BRIGHTON ATLANTICS
Jeremy Clarke

Perhaps of all the 20th century engines that came from its constituent companies to the Southern Railway in 1923, few could match for their looks those designed under the regime of Douglas Earle Marsh. The handsome 'Atlantics' did not possess the majestic bulk of Reid's on the North British - nor their appetite for coal! – nor the beautiful silhouette of Robinson's '8B' class on the Great Central, even in the case of the later 'H2s'. And yet there was something that made them particularly satisfying to the eye. (It was, I believe, the late Derek Cross who maintained the 4-4-2 wheel arrangement was the ideal provider of symmetry to a locomotive.)

Robert Billinton had been in charge of locomotive affairs at Brighton for fourteen years until his death in office on 7th November 1904 after a period of ill-health. He had continued Stroudley's standardisation ethos as well as the gamboge livery and the practice of naming every locomotive, no matter how small and insignificant it may have been. In 1892 he had introduced the neat 'D3' class 0-4-4T, whose outline was reproduced on LBSCR enginemen's cap badges for years afterwards, and from 1894 a range of handy 0-6-2 radial tank engines. Many of these lasted well into the BR era, though the prototype was Stroudley's 'West Brighton' of 1889, under construction at the time of his death. But Billinton's early express engines were seriously under-boilered. Though the later 'B4' class 4-4-0, which first came into traffic in December 1899, was an improvement, it was at best a mediocre performer. More seriously, plans Billinton had made for re-equipping Brighton Works had had to be held over due to the company's rather difficult financial position in the early years of the 20th century. Though matters had eased somewhat, the stringent financial situation had not been entirely resolved when Douglas Earle Marsh succeeded Billinton: he was officially appointed from 1st January 1905.

Born near Aylsham, North Norfolk, on 4th January 1862, little is known of Marsh's early life before, aged sixteen, he entered Brighton College. Did this early acquaintance with the LBSCR influence his decision to apply to succeed Billinton when the time came?

He began a premium apprenticeship at Swindon in October 1881 and eight years later was offered and accepted the post of Assistant Works Manager there. However, this turned out to be a very unhappy period in his professional life because his superior soon took a strong dislike to him, so much so that after the first few months there was no personal contact at all between them. However, that may have been in part due to Marsh's own temperament. He is generally recorded as being 'taciturn' and rather difficult to get on with. His troubled labour relations at Brighton may also point to this side of his character.

Towards the end of his time at Swindon the GWR suffered a serious accident on the main line through Cornwall. From 1887 Dean had turned out a series of twenty 0-4-2T engines which proved so unstable that a short-wheelbase four-wheel bogie was soon substituted for the pair of trailing wheels. But on 16th April 1895 two of these engines, double-heading an afternoon train from Plymouth, left the rails at 50mph on the curve between Doublebois and Bodmin Road. The pilot finished up against the cutting side while the train engine came to rest broadside across the track. Several of the leading vehicles were damaged but fortunately there were no fatalities and only fifteen people complained of injury. The Inspecting Officer considered misalignment of the track as one of the possible causes of the accident: two engines of the same class similarly double-heading had passed through only a little earlier. From another point of view this incident was directly responsible for Marsh's later dislike and distrust of front-coupled engines. It must therefore have much disturbed him when he went to Brighton to find both his predecessors had had no compunction about this, even on locomotives for fast train use. Stroudley's 'Gladstones' still bore much of such work and shed foremen were quite happy to allocate Billinton's larger wheeled 'E5' radial tanks to fast main line duties. Marsh later removed the leading coupling rods from a few of the 'radials' so that for a time they ran as 2-4-2T engines.

With a sense of relief no doubt Marsh left Swindon toward the end of 1895 to go to the Great Northern. He took up the post of Chief Assistant Mechanical Engineer of the company and Manager of Doncaster works under the new CME, Henry Ivatt. Both men officially began their GNR service at the beginning of 1896. By contrast with his Swindon experience Marsh had a quite harmonious working relationship with Ivatt, perhaps because the boss was a good delegator and therefore did not interfere directly in Marsh's domain. While at Doncaster he made a considerable contribution to the layout of 'The Crimpsall', the main locomotive erecting shop in the works. Because of his position, he also had much to do with the production and erection of the original and later Ivatt Atlantics, perhaps also with parts of the design. It was during his time with the GNR that, while on a fact-finding trip in Europe, he was shown the superheater patented by Wilhelm Schmidt, an

---

Opposite page - No 40, probably brand new. Compare with the sad appearance of the engine at the end on page 20. The air-brake only hose will be noted as will the link rather than a conventional screw-coupling.

An official view of No 421, later 'South Foreland' on the Crumbles siding at Eastbourne. The livery may well be umber rather than the more usual 'works grey' as might be seen in such images. Is that also a speedometer drive?

event having later significance in his work.

Marsh was one of four applicants for the post of Locomotive Superintendent at Brighton. Each man was invited to meet members of the Brighton Board separately, the meetings coincidentally taking place only two days after Billinton's death but obviously arranged earlier. (One unsuccessful interviewee, by-the-by, was Dugald Drummond's brother Peter, shortly to take up a similar position on the Highland Railway. He later claimed from the LBSCR the testimonials he had supplied and all the expenses incurred for his unsuccessful trip!) Marsh's appointment was confirmed shortly afterwards.

The Board had already expressed some concern about the general state of locomotive affairs and set up a sub-committee to look into them. Marsh made a report to that committee two months after taking office, stating that there was a substantial backlog of engines needing attention in the works as well as a need there for new equipment and a revision of the layout to improve efficiency. That being so any new locomotive construction would have to be contracted out until the situation improved. This decision was made against the background of a need for more powerful and up-to-date engines, and quickly.

Marsh's close connection with Ivatt's 'Atlantics' stemmed from the first introduction in 1898, but it was the larger-boilered version which arrived on the scene four years later that provided his prototype. Derek Cross argues, perhaps with some justification, that, besides the wheel arrangement, the wide-firebox and big boiler of this engine or those derived from it were not ideally suited to a railway where the longest main line run – Victoria to Portsmouth via the Mid-Sussex route – is less than ninety miles and most such journeys rather shorter than that. Also despite appearances, there are no 'easy' routes in the Brighton realm. London-Brighton itself features long climbs in both directions through the Downs and sharper gradients still on the later Quarry route. Besides these, down trains from London Bridge face 2¾ miles at 1 in 100 up to Forest Hill and there is the short but sharp 1 in 64 of Grosvenor bank off the platform end at Victoria, with no chance to gain much momentum. Several important junctions are subject to severe speed restrictions with an uphill gradient to follow, Keymer, for example, and Lewes.

One can understand why Marsh went for the familiar with the urgency of the need, particularly with the rising weight of trains on the introduction of heavier rolling stock. In the circumstances a six-coupled locomotive allied to, say, an improved Brighton 'B4' boiler might have been a better and cheaper solution. But Marsh at least recognised that, with the much denser traffic on the Brighton line, and

A most interesting view of H2 No B425 'Trevose Head' outside Victoria not long after grouping. The engine retains the original cab profile and the shapely chimney designed by Basil Field. The number has the 'B' prefix designating its Brighton origin, meaning this is before 1931 when 2000 was added instead. Add this information to the other detail and the date probably comes out around 1925/6. Note the none too straight smokebox handrail - see also lower view p12.

therefore, as well as closer station stops, the greater likelihood of signal checks, there was a need for good acceleration. In those circumstances the small 18¾"x 24" cylinders of the GNR engines would have to be enlarged.

It is certain Ivatt lent Marsh a complete set of the working drawings of his large Atlantics which accounts for the very marked similarities between the two designs. The coupled wheel diameters and rigid and overall wheelbases were exactly the same. While the cylinders were enlarged to 19" bore by 26" stroke (18½" in two of the first five) the boiler was virtually identical, though the LBSCR engines had a slightly deeper firebox. Grate area in both instances was 30.95 sq ft. The greatest difference was the working pressure, the 175psi of the GNR locos being increased to 200psi by Marsh, again one assumes in the interest of ensuring the crew had adequate power for brisk acceleration. Given that the heating surfaces were virtually identical, it might appear at first sight that Marsh was risking the capability of the boiler to make the necessary steam for the bigger cylinders. He must surely have been inculcated with Ivatt's dictum that 'a locomotive's success depends on its capacity to boil water' and in that respect the Ivatts could be deemed to be underboiled. As it was, the 5' 6" maximum diameter of the boiler and heating surface in

excess of 2400 sq ft was greater than anything seen on either railway up to the time of their introduction. The Ivatt engines were the heavier of the two though the difference was small, 68 tons 6 cwt against 67 tons exactly. However the Brighton engines unsurprisingly boasted a slightly greater adhesion weight, 37½ tons as against 36 tons. No doubt the much-increased nominal tractive effort, some 26% higher than that of the Great Northern locos, could account for the fact that the adhesion factor was slightly better than the ideal minimum of 4:1. (The 'Schools' by comparison had a very low figure of 3.74:1 which made gentle handling when starting away a necessity. I have seen drivers, with the engine in mid-gear, open the regulator and then wind the gear forward until the loco moved.)

The contract for the first five engines was let to Kitsons of Leeds, the small number in the order presumably a reflection of the Brighton's finances at the time. That assumption could have some truth to back it because the original agreed tender price of £3950 per engine was later reduced by £45 if each was delivered in grey primer rather than finished livery. Marsh may have concluded that Brighton Works could do the paint job more cheaply than Kitsons or, of course, he was as yet undecided on the livery to be adopted. 'H1' class No. 37 duly arrived in primer in

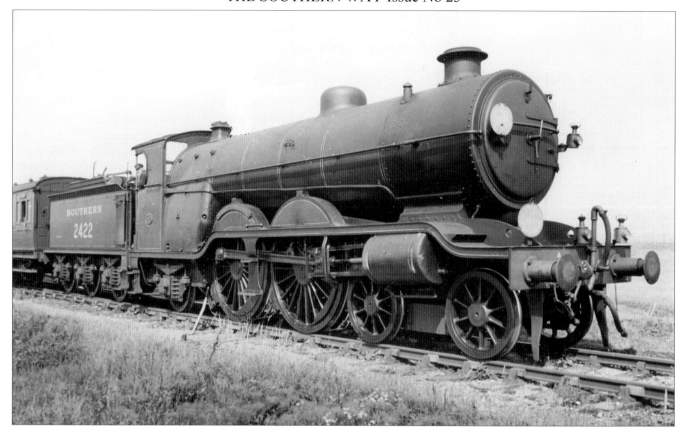

Above - H2 No 2422 'North Foreland' on shunt siding at Newhaven Harbour after working a boat train from Victoria, August 1937. C C B Herbert

Opposite top - Reported as being Brighton Steam Shed Staff, although more likely to have been men from the Drawing Office, or possibly the Outdoor Running Staff. The group are alongside H1 No 39 'La France'. 1921. The central figure (seated) with the spats is Lawson Billinton. A B McLeod.

Opposite bottom - H2 No 37 - later 'Selsey Bill'.

December 1905 and proceeded to run trials in it over the next few weeks. These trials were obviously satisfactory because Nos. 38-41 had arrived from Leeds without alteration by February 1906.

Other than the characteristic Billinton chimney the resemblance to the GNR engine was startling, even to the rise and fall of the footplate over the cylinders and the profile of and supports for the cab. Though the very distinctive Stroudley 'Improved Engine Green' provided a readily identifiable and distinctive look to Brighton engines it had become increasingly costly to apply. Hamilton Ellis also remarks 'one is not quite certain that this would have suited a really big engine'. Having essayed a dark green lined red and white Marsh settled on umber, edged dark brown and gold-lined black. (Billinton's son, Lawson, who succeeded Marsh in 1912, continued with it until Grouping). Moreover, to the further dismay of Brighton enthusiasts the naming of engines was generally discontinued.

By the time Marsh came to order the second batch of six engines from Brighton Works in 1910 he had, very probably at the prompting of his Chief Draughtsman, B K Field, made most successful use of the Schmidt superheater

in the excellent 'I3' class 4-4-2 tank engines. The first of these, No. 21, appeared in September 1907 and was unique in the class in being basically a tank engine version of Billinton's 'B4' 4-4-0. It was thus fitted with 6' 9" driving wheels. The coupled wheelbase also differed slightly from that of the other twenty-five 'I3s, which had the same 6' 7½" drivers as the Atlantics as well as several other common features.

Having built the first six of the I3 class with a superheater, Marsh left the next six saturated but carrying a higher boiler pressure in order to make a fair comparison. The economy of the superheated engines had rather more than a local impact. As a rule, the jointly-worked LBSCR/LNWR 'Sunny South Express', which loaded to around 250 tons, changed engines at Willesden Junction. But the North Western, fond of showing off its locomotives' prowess, confidently instigated the 'friendly' trials which saw the engines working through instead between Brighton and Rugby for a short period in November 1909. If nothing else the results convinced Marsh to install superheating on his main line engines thereafter as a matter of course. All the saturated 'I3s' were retro-fitted in time.

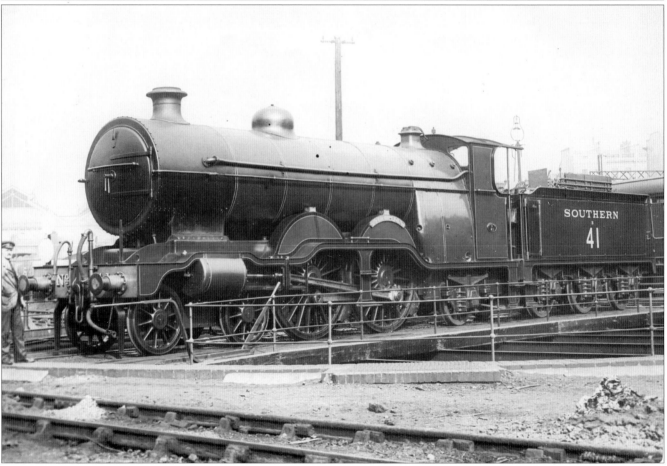

Top - *H2 No 2422 'North Foreland' in Southern green livery. The obvious difference in the framing above the cylinders between the two classes will be noted.*

Bottom - *No 41 'Peveril Point' seen soon after takeover by the SR. The number B41 lasted until 1931 when, to remove the anomaly of several engines potentially carrying the same numbers, the 'A', 'B' and 'E' prefixes were dropped and 1000 was added to SECR and 2000 to Brighton loco numbers. The view was taken on the turntable outside Victoria.*

THE BRIGHTON ATLANTICS

The Brighton's rival on the trials was one of George Whale's much vaunted 'Precursors', No. 7, 'Titan'. The North Western finished up here with egg on its corporate face for No. 23, with a water capacity of only 2110 gallons, was able to run the 90½ miles between East Croydon and Rugby without taking water. Consumption thus was only 23 gallons per mile at most. 'Titan' on the other hand had to pick up at Bushey troughs, something the Brighton engine was, of course, incapable of doing. With the bunker loaded to its absolute maximum of about 3¼ tons No. 23's coal consumption on a return Brighton-Rugby-Brighton journey could not exceed 27lbs per mile, under half of that regularly consumed by *Titan*. Cecil J Allen estimated this worked out at less than 0.1 lbs per ton-mile. No time was Brighton reached on return without some coal still left in the bunker, neither were the tanks ever completely emptied of water.

With the lesson so thoroughly learned, Crewe Works turned out Bowen Cooke's superlative – and superheated! - 'George the Fifth' class in 1910. (Was that a sore lesson one wonders? In his history of the LNWR that North Western *aficionado* O S Nock simply calls the 'George' a development of the 'Precursor' but refrains from giving any reason why or how that development came about.)

To return then to Brighton: as a result of his superheating results with the 'I3s' there were considerable changes in the 'H2' in the production and use of steam, not least the installation of a Schmidt superheater in all six engines. In addition the running board was tidied up, the smokebox now rested on a saddle and a new, massive though shapely chimney designed by Basil Field was applied. The cylinder diameter was enlarged to 21" but to sustain the tractive effort at about the same level as the earlier engines the pressure was reduced to 170psi, certainly an aid to boiler maintenance and a not unusual change at the time with superheating. The boiler heating surface came down by more than 400sq ft but the area of the superheater brought the total up to slightly more than the original. In all other mechanical and constructional respects the 'H2' was the same as the 'H1' though the weight went up, overall by 1½ tons, a ton of which was placed on the drivers.

By the time the class, numbered 421-6, arrived on scene - the first five late in 1911, the sixth early in 1912 - Marsh had retired after an extended period of sick leave and Lawson Billinton, who had held the fort *pro tem*, was in office. (Despite this period of ill-health, believed to be due to the pressures of his position, Marsh lived until 25th May 1933).

As might be expected, the Atlantics worked 'fast' services – the Brighton did not use the term 'express' – between its London termini and the main coastal towns, Brighton, Eastbourne, Bognor Regis and Portsmouth. They were also used to haul the all-Pullman 'Southern Belle' from its inception on 1st November 1908 when 'H1' no 39 was the engine concerned. This train ran daily, successor to

the 'Sunday Pullman Limited'. The latter had inaugurated the 'Brighton in Sixty Minutes' timing which continued with this new Pullman service and was to be the standard 'non-stop' time for years to come to/from both London termini, even in electrified days. (It should be noted the working time was generally less than this, varying between 55 and 58 minutes).

The Brighton was among those railways maintaining the practice of allocating an engine to one crew so daily mileage, by modern standards, was modest, even more so given the relatively short distances of the main routes and the frequency of services. (Two return London-Brighton trips were deemed a good day's work.) As a result the Atlantics did not have a monopoly of the best trains but worked turn and turn about with the 'I3s' and the two massive Pacific tanks of classes 'J1' and 'J2', arguably the most attractive engines to emanate from Brighton under Marsh. The 'J2' took the rails in February 1912 after Billinton was appointed, the first Brighton engine to be fitted with Walschaerts gear. However, the cylinder castings were the same as those used on the Atlantics and the 'J1', the steam chest between the frames thus requiring rocking levers to work the valves. Maskelyne remarks that that engine appeared to be livelier than her older sister, just as anecdotal evidence suggests the saturated 'H1' was a better performer than the superheated 'H2'. How much of that was due to its superior boiler pressure is questionable.

At Grouping four of the five 'H1's were allocated to Brighton shed with four of the 'H2s'. The fifth 'H1' was stationed at Battersea while Eastbourne shed had care of the remaining 'H2s'.

Only post-Grouping were changes made to the two classes. But before that event, and breaking Marsh's 'no name' code, No 39 became *La France* in 1913 in honour of the French Presidential visit to London that year. The engine retained this until all the 'Atlantics' were named by the Southern early in 1925. The late A B MacLeod, a Brighton man by training, told me in conversation he was given *carte blanche* by Richard Maunsell to choose the names, though I cannot recall if he said he was instructed to be thematic in his selection or why he chose those particular headlands around the South Coast. So it was that until withdrawal the Atlantics carried the following:

'H1'	37	Selsey Bill
	38	Portland Bill
	39	Hartland Point
	40	St Catherine's Point
	41	Peveril Point
'H2'	421	South Foreland
	422	North Foreland
	423	The Needles
	424	Beachy Head
	425	Trevose Head
	426	St Alban's Head

Knowing MacLeod's tidy engineering mind it

seems odd that the names appeared haphazardly rather than in order starting, for example, in East Kent at North Foreland and working around the coast to finish at Hartland Point in North Devon. The curved brass nameplates, 4⅜" wide, were attached directly to the top of rear driving wheel splashers. Contrary to GWR practice the 'T' of the two abbreviated 'Saint' names was the same size as the other letters. (The name *La France* incidentally followed Stroudley tradition in being hand-painted on the face of the rear splasher.)

In company with all other Brighton engines the Atlantics had their numbers prefaced by the letter 'B' after Grouping to signify their origins. This arrangement was superseded in 1931 when all ex-LBSCR engines had 2000 added to their numbers to do away with the nonsense of pre-Grouping number duplication. The umber livery was gradually lost too, the hue officially known as 'Maunsell Green' being introduced. This was a very slightly darker shade than the 'sage' used by Urie on the South Western. While on the subject of liveries, Bulleid introduced the bright 'Malachite Green' after 1937 and all the 'H2's together with 'H1' No 2038 were decked in it by 1947. It is doubtful if the engines retained the green throughout the war as the general use of unlined black was applied to virtually all locomotive stock. However, 'T9' No. 119, the Southern's 'Royal' engine, was certainly turned out in malachite for the duration. Post-nationalisation both classes were finished in BR lined black 'Mixed-traffic' livery which suited them quite well even if it couldn't compare favourably with Maunsell Green with Sunshine lettering!

Modest constructional changes to the engines came about following electrification of former LBSCR main lines though the 'H1s' had all been superheated between 1925 and 1927. Electric working to Brighton and Worthing (1st January 1933), to Eastbourne and Hastings (7th July 1935) and the Mid-Sussex line to Portsmouth, Bognor Regis and Littlehampton (3rd July 1938) left the Atlantics with little main line work other than boat trains to and from Newhaven Harbour.

The Brighton had the most generous loading gauge of all the Southern's pre-Grouping companies, so to increase the engines' route availability from this time the eaves on the cab roof of all eleven were trimmed and radiused while the centre of the roof itself was lowered and the whistle removed from it. The other obvious change was to do with the chimney where both the Billinton and Field versions were superseded by the squatter Maunsell type as fitted to his 3-cylinder 'Moguls'. The overall result was not displeasing.

As well as these structural alterations the boiler pressure of the 'H2' class was raised to 200psi, providing a commensurately sharp rise in nominal tractive effort. Maunsell superheaters had been fitted to the 'H1s', the 'H2s' receiving these as they passed through shops in place of the Schmidt type. Maunsell's had a rather smaller surface area but its connections at the headers provided a less restrictive passage for steam and made the fittings easier to remove.

By 1938 and following the structural changes, four Atlantics had been transferred to Stewarts Lane to work

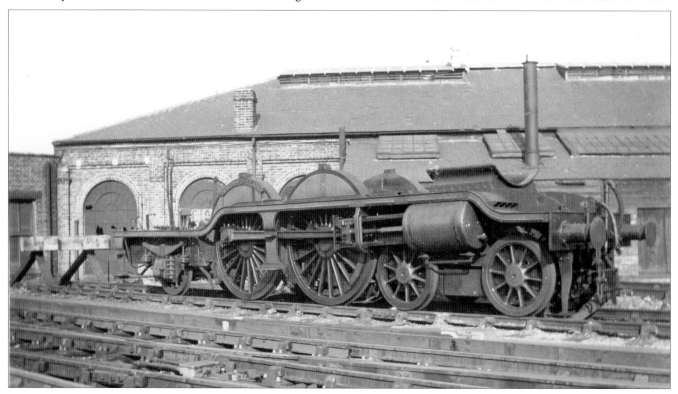

Frames and motion from H2 No 2422 'North Foreland; outside Brighton Works. H M Madgwick.

No 2040 'St Catherines Point' leaving Chichester on a London Bridge to Portsmouth excursion, 17 April 1938.

K O B Nicols

London-Ramsgate trains but the remaining seven were still on home ground, five at New Cross Gate, two at Newhaven. Wartime saw several moves into other 'foreign' territory. First though, all the London-based engines were sent to Brighton in 1939 but the seaside sojourn for seven of them was short-lived as they were back at New Cross by early 1940. Generally kept for special traffic, the nightly London Bridge-Brighton newspaper train formed their only regular duty, returning with a morning parcels train after rush hour. Later that year all six 'H2s' were allocated to Basingstoke for semi-fast Waterloo-Salisbury and Reading-Portsmouth services. Three years later the six were to be found at Ashford for local work and secondary main line duties to/from Charing Cross.

The 'H1s', all five of which had stayed on home ground, were showing signs of age, no doubt exacerbated by patchy maintenance due to the demands of wartime working. Nos. 40 and 41 were withdrawn in January and March 1944 respectively, the latter being cut up almost straightaway while the former was stored in the open at Eastleigh until 1948. It is tempting to speculate that this engine was to be used as a bank of spare parts but I have found no evidence to support that. And if so, why Eastleigh rather than Brighton?

The saving grace for the remaining nine engines

was the resumption of boat trains to/from Newhaven in 1945: no larger engine could be dealt with at Newhaven shed. On the other side of the coin these were now among the heaviest workings the classes had ever been called upon to undertake. At the height of summer, loadings often reached twelve coaches and at least one van, a total tare weight of around 400 tons.

The next Atlantic to go, 'H2' No. 32423, was withdrawn in May 1949 by which time the Bulleid / Raworth Co-Co electric engines of 1941/45 vintage had taken over the principal boat train working, ousting the two 'Schools' class locos intended for it and thus allocated to Newhaven in 1945. Those engines had not been in the best of condition which meant the Atlantics often had to be used instead. Nevertheless, the 4-4-2s continued to work the relief boat services, many of which were quite as weighty as the main train.

Among their other allocated duties at this time were London-Uckfield-Brighton services. As Derek Cross remarked, the hilly Oxted route through the Downs made the main Brighton line appear as flat as a billiard table. But he writes enthusiastically of a covert footplate ride in 1950 on No. 32425, *Trevose Head*, in charge of the 4.40pm from London Bridge to Brighton via Oxted. He comments that the engine rode 'like a Rolls-Royce.......the best riding

Believed to have been taken at Stewarts Lane. In the cab are Fitter W Brooks and Assistant L Thomas. On the ground: Fitter A Martin, Shop Officeman Sid Norman (whose title was known to cover a multitude of responsibilities), and Fitters Assistant L Penfold. The engine is H2 No 32424 'Beachy Head'.

example, were common on the line until at least the mid-fifties.

Despite this praise Cross still holds to his view the engines 'were probably the wrong concept for the lines over which they had to work'. The Oxted line, with its long gradients at 1 in 100 and a very difficult start southbound off the platform end at Lingfield might well fall within the bounds of that comment. (In that light one wonders why the plodding Midland 2P class 4-4-0s with 7'0½ driving wheels – 6'9" in the LMS variety - were for years considered suitable motive power for local and piloting work on the Somerset & Dorset line north of Evercreech with its miles of 1 in 50 gradient).

The eight-strong Atlantic allocation toward the end of 1950 was: Nos. 32037/8, New Cross Gate: Nos. 32039/425/6, Brighton: Nos. 32421/2/4, Newhaven. By this time too and for some years afterwards the engines were regularly seen on Inter-Regional workings to and from the South Coast, Kensington (Addison Road/Olympia) being the usual changeover point. Here again some very heavy trains, of up to 400 tons, were entrusted to them with some difficult climbs to be overcome even before leaving the London area. The speed-restricted upward and reverse-curved sweep from Latchmere Junction to Falcon Junction, for example, came before the engine was really warmed up. This is immediately followed by the near two miles up to Balham and then the short but sharp rise between Streatham and Norbury, all making for some skilled and thoughtful driving.

The Newhaven-based engines also had regular duties on Oxted line commuter services. Among these were the 0821 Lewes-London Bridge and 1740 back via East Grinstead, and the 0818 Uckfield-Victoria and 1810 return, the 'Terrible 6.10'! The trains were smartly timed, particularly over the electrified suburban sections of the route north of South Croydon and, as noted earlier, there were some quite difficult starts away from intermediate stations in both directions.

By 1951, however, the influx of Brighton-built LMS Fairburn 2-6-4T engines had taken over the bulk of the work on the 'Oxted Group' including those south of Tunbridge Wells and East Grinstead to Lewes and Eastbourne. Further inroads were made that year into Atlantic numbers with the withdrawal of the three remaining 'H1s'. No. 39 went in February, having been used as a guinea pig to test the sleeve valves planned for Bulleid's 'Leader' class, and Nos. 37 and 38 in July. Marsh's beautiful 'J' class 'Pacific' tank engines were also taken out of service in June that year from Brighton shed, their duties having been usurped by the Fairburns. All the 'I3s' but one (No. 24, w/d 11/44) came into BR ownership but they too were withdrawn between January 1950 and April 1952. The last out was the last in, No. 91 having entered service in March 1913: it was broken up at Ashford in January 1953.

The five 'H2s' still active were split between Newhaven (3) and Brighton (2), this pair often having the

locomotive on which I have been'. The gradients between South Croydon and his destination at Oxted were tackled 'as if they didn't exist. There was no noise, no hustle, just a steady, strong pull all the way'.

He also remarks on the skill of the fireman whom he calls a near-genius, for the firing was constant but not heavy, half-shovelsful of coal going on to 'a thin fire dancing on the grate and with the needle always on the red line'. Regrettably he gives no specific details of the make-up or weight of the train beyond the fact it was 'heavy'. The likelihood is it consisted of between seven and nine coaches, a tare weight of between say 200 and 260 tons, given that lighter pre-Grouping stock regularly appeared on such workings at this time. Ex-SECR 'Birdcage' sets, for

No 32424 'Beachy Head' at Tulse Hill. The train is coming off the 1869 spur from Herne Hill and bearing the post-Nationalisation No 20 headcode. So far as it applies to this train it is scheduled to run 'via Streatham Spur' but there is nothing beyond that. (Probably it would be changed for a more specific one at a suitable location, possibly East Croydon.) The stock is obviously London Midland, which suggests from the location shown the train came off the ex-Midland line and took the Brent Curve and the 'Midland Goods Line' to the North & South Western Junction Joint line to Kew East Junction and thence to the Windsor side of Clapham Junction where engines would have been changed. Thence Ludgate Junction, Factory Junction, ex-LCDR to Herne Hill. The Brighton main line would have been joined at Streatham Common. As there is a reporting number on the disc at the centre of the bufferbeam, this is probably as excursion rather than a regularly timetabled service though if it were a Summer Saturday that likelihood would not necessarily hold true. If the former, Brighton would be the obvious destination. A Summer Saturday working was most likely extended to Eastbourne and possibly Hastings, though the whole train would not work beyond Brighton. I know this all sounds a bit vague but may be a pointer.

Brighton-Bournemouth and Brighton-Plymouth trains among their duties, the latter being taken as far as Portsmouth. Despite their age they remained popular with crews and enthusiasts alike. The RCTS organised an ambitious tour on 6th February 1955 which started with a leg from Waterloo to Guildford in the hands of a Brighton Atlantic, in this case No. 32421, *South Foreland*. The Nine Elms crew to man it consisted of Driver Hooker and Fireman Botton.

Bert Hooker recounts in his autobiography that his

H2 No 32426 'St Albans Head' at Bricklayers Arms, 20 February 1952. The blackened numbers on the smokebox plate will be noted. J F W Paige

only previous acquaintance with the class was as a cleaner at New Cross Gate before the war. He also comments that Bill Botton was probably the only fireman at Nine Elms who had had any experience with these engines, perhaps the reason why he got the duty. Bert Hooker's cousin, Ernest King, had transferred from Slade Green to Newhaven following electrification of the routes to Dartford in 1926, and was thus both familiar with and enthusiastic about the class. Bert commented he was about to find out how much the engine lived up to the reputation his cousin gave it.

South Foreland had been brought up to Stewarts Lane shed where Bert and his mate prepared it. Having run light to Waterloo the crew were then advised that such had been the demand for tickets the train was now one of ten coaches weighing, according to the guard, 360 tons. Routed via Brentford and Chertsey, the organisers were now concerned about whether the engine was capable of lifting this heavy train up the Byfleet curve from Addlestone Junction. Like any good engineman Bert had already assessed the problem and assured them 'we would be alright'. It is worth recounting his record of the running at this point. "[Addlestone Junction distant].... signal was at caution. I slowed right down, the home signal was lowered, then the starter – the Atlantic moving at about 10 mph. I had advanced the lever to about 50% cut off with just a breath of steam going through the cylinders. All eyes on the

distant signal for Byfleet Junction, two or three hundred yards from it and it dropped 'off', full first regulator, then a touch of the big valve and 32421 jumped to it, downhill past the distant, under the main line, then we were going uphill on a right-hand curve on to the down local line. The old girl seemed to swoop around the curve and as the train entered it, it perceptively slowed as the gradient and the flange drag took their toll. Full regulator now but she 'had them' and emerged triumphantly on to the down local line. My mate had done his stuff, the Ramsbottom safety valves were buzzing and the water was kept well in sight in the gauge glass".

Many years later Bert Hooker remembered this trip very well. No engineman liked to stop his train if he could possibly help it and Bert was no exception. Questioned during conversation about what he would have done had the Byfleet 'distant' remained stubbornly at 'caution' he said 'kept going at no more than walking pace. But if I had to stop I'd have done so at least one hundred yards before the signal. That would have given me a good downhill run to get some momentum'. As he had said at the time, the problem had been assessed and plans laid.

That doyen of recorders, Cecil J Allen, has published a number of runs on the Brighton line with both classes. One of the earliest features an 'H1', No. 41, in non-superheated condition at the head of the 5.pm from London

Bridge. The train is a substantial one of 325 tons gross to be run on the standard sixty-minute non-stop timing. New Cross Gate was passed in 4¾ minutes from the start at 54mph though the 2¾ miles at 1 in 100 up to Forest Hill brought this down to 40mph. The fifteen minute timing from the start to East Croydon was cut by almost a minute and despite speed falling to 41mph up the long 1 in 264 climb to the summit at mp 17¼, the train was still a minute early at Quarry box. Being nicely inside time the driver took things fairly easily down the subsequent grades, a maximum of 69mph being recorded at both Horley and Haywards Heath. Even so the train was no less than 2¾ minutes ahead of time at Keymer Junction and despite a signal check the summit at the south end of Clayton tunnel was cleared at 46mph. Arrival at Brighton was 1¼ minutes early. Allen estimates the nett time to be 57¾ minutes.

Two trips non-stop from Victoria show the work of the 'H2' though the first, with No. 421 hauling 325 tons, began badly, the engine stalling on the 1 in 64 to Grosvenor bridge. Although rear end assistance arrived relatively quickly the train was nearly 11½ minutes late through Clapham Junction and only seconds had been recovered by the time it passed East Croydon. Allen comments that in the circumstances a higher speed than 43mph might have been expected at mp 17¼ but thereafter the driver opened up. Horley was passed at 80½ mph and the summit at Balcombe tunnel was surmounted at a minimum of 54mph. All but 80mph was attained at Keymer Junction, by which time the lateness had been reduced to 7¼ minutes, and with a final 66mph at Patcham arrival at Brighton was only seven minutes late. The 48.2 miles from Clapham Junction had been covered at a very creditable average of 57½ mph pass-to-stop. Allen calculates the nett time as 56 minutes.

On the second of these two runs No. 422 was faced with a load of no less than 405 tons gross. The time of 2 mins 12 secs from the start to Grosvenor bridge suggests some rear-end assistance may have been provided, even if it were only the length of the platform, particularly given the times achieved over other rising sections of the route. For example, the 1 in 165 rise to Balham brought the speed down from 45mph at Clapham Junction (passed 54 seconds late) to 37mph and the short but quite sharp climbs from Streatham to Norbury and Thornton Heath to Selhurst probably caused the loss of a further minute to East Croydon. The load told on the rate of acceleration up the ensuing 1 in 264 from the speed restriction there, but the summit at mp 17¼ was nevertheless passed at an excellent 41mph though the train was still two minutes late at Quarry.

Whether the engine was winded by the exertion is impossible to know but in view of the lateness one would have expected a higher speed at Horley than 72½mph. Perhaps the mortgaged boiler needed some recovery or the driver was saving something for the next long climb, from Gatwick to Balcombe tunnel, for the train passed the tunnel box at no less than 50mph. Such an effort had its rewards for by Keymer Junction, passed at 74mph, the lateness was a

The former No 39 'La France' subsequently renamed 'Hartland Point' and seen as Southern No 2039 during the time it was running with sleeve valves reference Bulleid's 'Leader' class experiment.

mere twenty seconds. After another brisk sprint through Patcham, Brighton was reached three seconds early, overall an excellent performance with this load. With no significant checks Allen considered the nett time to be the same as the actual one.

CJA also describes three up direction runs though the engines concerned were not nearly as heavily loaded as those going down. Once more 'H1' No. 41 in its saturated condition features, though on this occasion the load was only 200 tons gross. In these circumstances it was not surprising that time was being gained consistently, so much so that signals checked progress at Earlswood and particularly at East Croydon. Nevertheless, No. 41 was still two minutes early at Balham and an uninterrupted run from

The end for No 2040, 'St Catherines Point'. Withdrawn in January 1944 and awaiting breaking up.

there brought the train into Victoria 3½ minutes before time.

The second of these runs was made by 'H2' No. 422 hauling 265 tons gross. Not to put too fine a point on it the start was electrifying. At the end of the initial 1 in 264 off the platform end at Brighton to the south end of Clayton tunnel at mp46 No. 422 was already a minute up on No. 41. Another ½ minute had been gained to Keymer Junction, passed at 74mph, and though the following climb to Balcombe Tunnel box was surmounted at 56½mph against the 58½ of No. 41, No. 422 had almost achieved 'even time' by Earlswood, the 29 miles being covered in 29 mins 22 secs. The train was three minutes early here. Despite much easier running from Balcombe to Quarry, and even more so down the gradient through Purley, signals at East Croydon checked the train so severely No. 422 was a minute later than No. 41 through Balham. Further checks were experienced at Clapham Junction, the arrival at Victoria being only a ¼ minute early. Allen calculated the nett time at 53¾ minutes.

The final run was taken by 'H2' No. 426, the load here being 300 tons gross. This run started well with the train passing Keymer Junction dead on time at 74mph. But a preceding laggard then checked it as far as Balcombe Tunnel Junction before it could be turned on to the slow line. The delays saw No. 426 pass Three Bridges 3½ minutes late. Some very fast running followed with 54mph at Quarry box and no less than 75mph at Purley. The 50mph restriction at East Croydon was slightly exceeded

though the train was still 1½ minutes late here. A determined effort followed however, Balham being passed only ¼ minute late with an exceptional speed of 71½mph recorded at Wandsworth Common. The train was thus through Clapham Junction ¾ minute ahead of schedule. But for a final check on the approaches Victoria would have been reached in about 58½ minutes. As it was, the final stop was made in 59¾ minutes though the nett was reckoned to be 5½ minutes less than this. One comment Allen makes concerning the last run is that the actual time for the 10.85 miles from Purley to Clapham Junction was only 10 mins 29 secs, something of a rarity over this section at an average of 62mph. He also makes the point that, but for the final signal check, the 29.55 miles from Three Bridges to Victoria would have taken only just over thirty minutes. Furthermore, he notes that the nett times on all three runs are inside the fifty-five minute schedule of the non-stop electrics at the time he was writing. As a matter of interest there are no non-stop workings now but 'Southern' still manages a half-hourly service in both directions taking just 52 minutes with calls at both Clapham Junction and East Croydon on the way. Such is progress!

The same year the RCTS trip was made something occurred well away from the Brighton line that would spell the end for four of the remaining five engines. On 1st September 1955 the Eastern Region 'W1' class 4-6-4 no 60700 suffered a bogie frame failure leaving Peterborough station, leading to derailment. All bogies of similar design

Leading Dimensions (as built)	H1	H2
Cylinders (2) diameter	19"	21"
Stroke	26"	26"
Driving Wheel diameter	6' 7 ½"	6' 7 ½"
Wheelbase, rigid	6' 10"	6' 10"
" total	26' 4"	26' 4"
Heating surface, tubes	2,337 sq ft	1,913 sq ft
Heating surface, firebox	136 sq ft	137 sq ft
Total evaporative	2,473 sq ft	2,050 sq ft
Superheating surface	-	461 sq ft
Grate area	30.95 sq ft	30.95 sq ft
Working pressure	200lbs psi	170lbs psi
Tractive effort (85%BP)	20,060lbs	20,840lbs
Adhesion weight	38½ tons	38½ tons
Weight in working order	67 tons	68½ tons
Tender capacity – coal	4 tons	4 tons
- water	3500 gals	3500 gals
Weight full	39 tons	39 tons
Weight, engine & tender	106 tons	107½ tons

and construction thus came under scrutiny, those of the 'H2s' among them. Four of these, on Nos. 32421/2/5/6, were found to have similar faults. While the engine that induced the scrutiny was fitted with a new bogie and survived until June 1959, the cost of re-equipping the Atlantics could not be justified because of their age. The four were withdrawn from Brighton shed in August and September 1956. However Brighton continued to find work for No. 32424, generally on parcels or mail workings, though those became increasingly spasmodic. Even when the final call came, the engine was not allowed to slip quietly away. On 24th April 1958, en route to Eastleigh for scrapping, 'Beachy Head', specially cleaned by the staff at Brighton shed, worked a train from Lancing to Micheldever, twelve coaches of empty stock, a substantial load in excess of 375 tons. There was life in the old dog yet!

Attempts to preserve this, the final working Atlantic engine in the country, failed. Had it lasted perhaps even only two more years, by which time the preservation movement in general had gained more strength, the outcome might have been different. But *Laus Deo*, in the late 1990s

the Bluebell Railway, in the heart of former LBSCR territory, purchased an ex-GNR Atlantic boiler to go with other acquired parts of former Brighton engines with a view to recreating an 'H2', No. 32424 no less, a project now well underway.

Bibliography

British Atlantic Locomotives,
Cecil J Allen, Ian Allan Ltd, 1976.
Douglas Earle Marsh, His Life and Times,
Klaus Marx, The Oakwood Press, 2005.
The London, Brighton & South Coast Railway,
C Hamilton Ellis, Ian Allan Ltd., 1960.
Locomotives I Have Known,
J N Maskelyne, Percival Marshall, 1959.
Locomotives Illustrated, No. 37, The Larger Brighton Locomotives, Ian Allan Ltd., 1984.
Southern Railway Liveries,
Brian Haresnape, Ian Allan Ltd., 1982.
Nameplates of the Big Four,
Frank Burridge, Guild Publishing, 1985.

Pre-Grouping Southern Steam in the 1950s,
Peter Hay, Ian Allan Ltd., 1983.
Southern Region Steam Album,
S C Nash, Ian Allan Ltd., 1974.
The Croydon, Oxted & East Grinstead Railway,
David Gould, The Oakwood Press, 2003.
The Changing Southern Scene, 1948-1981,
Michael Baker, Ian Allan Ltd., 1981.
Nine Elms Engineman,
A E 'Bert' Hooker, Bradford Barton, (undated).
Bert Hooker, Legendary Engineman,
Oxford Publishing Co., 1994.
The London & North Western Railway,
O S Nock, Ian Allan Ltd., 1960.
Locomotives Illustrated, No. 170,
An LNER Miscellany, Ian Allan Ltd., 2008.
Railway Track Diagrams No. 5,
Southern & TfL, TRACKmaps, 3rd edition, 2008.
Table of Distances, LBSCR, January 1901,
(Reproduction, Ian Allan Ltd.,).
British Rail Main Line Gradient Profiles,
Ian Allan Ltd., (undated).
'Railway Liveries, Southern Railway,
Brian Haresnape, Ian Allan Ltd., 1982'.

*Atlantic detail on No 2421 'South
Foreland' recorded at Newhaven (Harbour /
Pier?) in 1947.*

C C B Herbert

BRIGHTON TO BOURNEMOUTH ON AN ATLANTIC

Of all the remaining veteran locomotives which are still at work in Britain today, none has greater popular appeal than the last five engines of the Atlantic type in these islands - the Marsh engines of the erstwhile London Brighton and South Coast Railway.

Almost everyone knows how Douglas Earle Marsh came to Brighton from Doncaster and gave that railway the benefit of Ivatt's excellent design for a top-ranking express locomotive. Certain modifications were made in the Brighton engines, as compared with their Great Northern forebears; the cylinders were given a longer stroke – 26 in. instead of 24 in. and the boiler barrel was nearly 10 inches longer between tube plates. In the second batch of engines, classified "H2," which alone survive, the cylinders were 21 inches diameter and 26 inches stroke, and the boilers were equipped with superheaters. The working pressure was the same as that of the Doncaster engines, 170 p.s.i., but in 1938 this was raised to 200 p.s.i. The footplating at the rear end was longer than that on the Great Northern Atlantics, with the result that a more comfortable cab provided more room for the enginemen.

It has always been said that the Brighton engines were never quite so good as the Doncaster engines, and the longer stroke of the cylinders has been held to be the reason. Certainly on the Great Northern main line there were many more opportunities for running than were ever possible on the short main lines of the Brighton, and there were many more and heavier trains to be worked. Apart from the L.N.W. "George V" class, I doubt if any 4-coupled engines have ever been called upon to handle consistently such huge long-distance trains as were the Great Northern Atlantics. The most arduous duties of the Brighton engines, on the other hand, were the Newhaven boat trains, which duties these old engines were still able to do until comparatively recently, though in the past six years their duties have mainly been confined to the relief boat trains in the summer month

Since the summer of 1951 the Atlantics, now all shedded at Brighton, have mostly been used only when required for special trains, or when there has been a shortage of other motive power The most arduous duties these 46-year-old engines have recently been called upon to perform have been the Brighton to Bournemouth trains. They have appeared on these turns on several occasions, and through the kind co-operation of the Motive Power Superintendent. Mr T. E. Chrimes, it was arranged that I should travel to Bournemouth and back on one of them. The day was a fine warm Saturday in early October, the engine was No. 32421 *South Foreland* and the train were the 9.40 am from Brighton to Bournemouth West, and the return the 1.10 p.m. Bournemouth West to Brighton. I was on the end of the long curving No 2 platform at Brighton when the engine backed on to the train, and a very pretty sight she was. The cleaners had done a good job, for not only was she spotless externally, but the cab also had been cleaned and polished, and I could not help thinking that honour had been done me that day. As I have said, the cabs of these engines are much more commodious than were those of the Ivatt engines, but the reverser, which is of the screw type, assisted by a compressed air cylinder, comes far back in the cab. The driver has a wood seat over the top of the cut-off indicator, and when the position of the gear is altered he needs must get off his seat and move to the rear of the cab to do it.

The steam pressure gauge is located on the inside of the cab sheets on the fireman's side. I have heard it said that as many Brighton engines were poor steamers, the gauge was so placed in order that it should be well away from the driver's critical eye! If this is so, then I think that, in the case of the Atlantics, it was a most unnecessary precaution. A feature of Brighton engines is the high position of the tender shovel plate. This is placed at a higher level than is the firehole door, so that the fireman never has to *lift* the coal, only carry it, on the shovel, across the cab. I am delighted that the Brighton Atlantics in their old age have never been fitted with pop safety valves. So, when they blow off, and they often do, one hears the characteristic hum of the Ramsbottom valves. A pleasant sound, but one which, like the fluctuating hum of the steam-driven threshing machine, is now almost no more than a nostalgic memory.

Our train for Bournemouth was made up of modern Southern stock - eight bogies of 262½ tons tare (this was given to Driver Charles Wood as 291 tons) and not far short of 300 tons gross. The train was very full and there was a great deal of heavy luggage. Wood said that usually he had a "West Country" on this duty, and although the Atlantics had worked the train on occasions during the summer, No 32421 had been in store for four weeks.

In front of the tender we had some excellent coal and fireman W. Bolingbroke had little to do for the first fifty miles that day.

Leaving Brighton on time, with the engine blowing off, Wood made a gentle start with half regulator and the reverser soon brought to 30 per cent, for the six miles downhill at an average of 1 in 378. Surely there are few termini which can offer such an excellent start to "cold" engines. The shed staff turned out to see us on our way, and then we were in the short tunnel, and running easily in the forties through Hove and on to Worthing. Top speed was 52½ m.p.h. near Southwick, after which the regulator was shut when we saw Lancing distant at yellow. It cleared, and we made Worthing on time.

With a full train and many travellers at each station it was unavoidable that the time allowed at stations should be exceeded, and so it was at most of the stops we made. Leaving Worthing ¾minute late, Wood soon had the engine working with full regulator and 30 per cent cut-off along a road which has the contours of a very gentle switchback, until Fareham is reached, 47½ miles from the start. It was, however, soon quite obvious that our eight-coach train was about as much as the engine would comfortably handle. Even from Worthing the start was very sluggish and I noticed that full fore gear was now arranged to give 66 per cent cut-off. Wood also had decided views that the engine needed more lead on the valves, and after spending nearly six hours on the footplate, during which time we stopped and started some thirty times, I should think he was probably right. But it was a pleasure now to be on such an easily riding machine, and to have no worries about steam.

We lost a little time to Arundel Junction which was taken very cautiously, and after this, full regulator and 40 per cent, were used, against full boiler pressure, to take the train to Barnham. Maximum was 41 m.p.h. along the level after passing Ford, where we met one of the huge Southern electric engines travelling on the other line with a train of empty wagons. At Barnham, the train was nearly 2¾ minutes late and extended time at the platform put us another ½-minute in arrears by the time the train left. On the 6¼ easy miles to Chichester, the nine-minute allowance proved too tight for us, and largely as a result of slow acceleration, we dropped another ½-minute. Maximum was a sustained 57 m.p.h. at Drayton and full regulator with 40 per cent was used all the way.

At Chichester, the tender tank was replenished inside the three minutes allowed - a very fine piece of work on the part of Wood and Bolingbroke, and the train left, three minutes and twenty seconds late, for the longest non-stop run of the journey - the 33 miles to Southampton Central, for which the time allowance is 47 minutes. We got away very well and soon were working in 35 per cent, with, as usual, full regulator. The valve was a bit heavy and stiff and it took the combined efforts of both men to get the regulator fully open. The engine was blowing off most of the way, but still we lost time and were nearly five minutes late passing Havant, after which we had signals against us and a bad p.w. check at Bedhampton, where the level crossing gates were under repair. There was no time to achieve real speed before we came, now nearly 6 minutes late, to Farlington Junction, where they make corsets and where the Southampton line branches to the right and leaves the electrified Brighton line to Portsmouth. This is, from now on, old South Western territory and the riding of the engine at once became easier. There is no doubt that the electric trains make for very rough track. Once we had cleared the junction, full regulator and a little more than 35 per cent cut-off took the train along at 50 mph. There was still plenty of steam, though by now the coal was getting decidedly dusty and Bolingbroke was having to work much harder. Even so, it wan necessary to fire the engine only six times between Brighton and Fareham (pass), a distance of 47½, miles.

We went cautiously through Fareham and then 32421 was opened up again on the rising gradients culminating in a mile at 1 in 70 before Swanwick. Full regulator and 35 per cent, got the speed up to 44 mph at the bottom of the 1 in 70 and then, increasing to 45 per cent, Wood got his train over the top with a minimum of 38½ m.p.h. and the engine sounding as if she really meant business. Then, with steam shut off, the running was very cautious down to Bursledon and afterwards the driving was beautifully controlled along a tortuous and difficult route which winds along the interesting banks of the river Itchen. We had a clear road all the way, and as we swung round the curves at St. Denys and ran along to Northam Junction we were the object of much interest among railwaymen and civilians alike. Through the tunnels we went, with the safety valves humming merrily, to draw up in Southampton Central only 4¼ minutes late. From Cosham, the old engine had picked up a few minutes and had given me a most pleasant and comfortable ride, full of interest and with the lovely weather helping to add to my pleasure. It is probable, too, that most of the time we were in arrears could be attributed to the Bedhampton slack. Again the train overstayed its station allowance, and we left 5 minutes late. For the next 13½ miles to Brockenhurst we made a very bright run, and the Atlantic seemed on this section to be at her best. Again we went with full regulator for most of the way and the cut-off at 35 per cent. After passing Lyndhurst Road speed rose to 57 at Beaulieu Road and to 61 m.p.h. on the short down-grade immediately afterwards. The train drew into Brockenhurst in 10 seconds less than schedule time from Southampton.

The start on the 1 in 176 up towards Sway was surprisingly easy and full regulator and maximum cut-off -55 per cent took the engine up past Lymington Junction at 30 m.p.h. in quite a thrilling manner, though for the first time the boiler was showing signs of feeling the strain, the fire was getting dirty and pressure fell to 180 lb. We came to New Milton and for some reason this station is a most awkward place for down trains. I never remember a call here without having to "draw up" and the engine always seems to be on a "dead centre." So it was today and all but three minutes elapsed before we got away. In the 5.8 miles to Christchurch, however, we achieved our highest speed of the whole

journey - 63½ m.p.h. at Hinton Admiral. The engine rode very quietly at this speed, and in fact on all occasions her movement never approached the amplitude of that for which the Great Northern engines were noted. For all the gallant dash this engine was no sinecure on a stopping train and the three stops before Bournemouth was reached were a great trial. Because of the limited cut-off, the lack of adequate lead, or what you will everywhere we had to set back and from being but 4½ minutes late arriving at New Milton, we were nearly 9½ minutes late into Bournemouth Central - a loss of all but 5 minutes in 9½ miles, with a dirty fire and pressure on the wane.

The Atlantic left the train at the Central station - it was taken on to Bournemouth West by a 'T9' - and I went thankfully to attend to the needs of the inner man, before travelling on myself to the West station for the return journey.

The return working to Brighton leaves Bournemouth West at 1.50 p.m. and is allowed three hours and four minutes, with seventeen stops instead of the ten on the outward journey. The same train is used. The men take the engine from the Central station to the sub-depot at Branksome where, after turning on the triangle, it is coaled, watered, serviced and the fire cleaned. The men have their food and get back on to the train at West station, all within an hour and a half. The old Atlantic came down the bank to the station with plenty of time to spare, and as she backed on to the train, was the centre of attraction for many railwaymen and passengers. It was something of an anti-climax, therefore, when we had to set back twice before she would take the train away and up the 1 in 90 to the West Junction. She was hard to reverse with pressure in the steam chests and the fact that the air cylinder, which assists in reversing, was out of action was a great handicap. However, we got going at last and with full regulator and full cut-off we awoke the echoes of Branksome with our efforts. In spite of the fact that the engine was definitely not the type to choose for a stopping train, to begin with we did remarkably well, adhering very closely to schedule. The start on the 1 in 119 up at Hinton Admiral caused some trouble - we set back, slipped very violently and had to set back again before finally moving the train in the right direction, and we then drove nearly all the way to New Milton with full regulator and 55 per cent cut-off. Wood remarked that the "Atlantics no longer liked the banks."

Nevertheless, we ran in many places at 60 m.p.h. and reached Southampton virtually on time - a very fine effort with a fire which although it had been cleaned at Branksome, was again becoming dirty, and the usual dirty slack and dust in the tender. The good coal we had started with from Brighton that morning had long since been used. We set out from Southampton with the engine blowing off, and we went well through the tunnel to Northam Junction and then got held outside St. Denys for 2¼ minutes while a dilatory local for Eastleigh stood on the down main platform. It was apparently just foul of the junction locks

Bottom - The same engine, but now British Railways No 32421 waiting departure from Bournemouth Central with the afternoon through train to Brighton. 5 July 1951.   *N Ewart Mitchell*

and not until it went on its way could we cross behind it, and into the Fareham line platform, 3¼ minutes late. Our start on the check-railed curve, up at 1 in 155, was also very difficult but at Woolston, the next station, where the start is on a curve and a gradient of 1 in 97 against the engine, the old lady went away like a bird with no slip and no need to set back.   Maybe she did so just to prove miracles sometimes happen.   For the fireman had said to me it would be "a ruddy miracle if we get away from here without a lot of bother." So on to Netley and down through Bursledon and then to tackle the 1 in 81 up to Swanwick.   With the regulator fully open 40 per cent cut-off, we were doing 36 m.p.h. at the bottom of the climb and 29 m.p.h. at Swanwick, where the gradient eases to 1 in 251. With a maximum of 50 m.p.h. down the other side, we came slowly into Fareham station.   Here they held us for more than five minutes while some shunting took place at the back of the train, and a horsebox attached. This incident remains in my mind, because of the long time which was needed for the operation and the fact that on the footplate we were in complete ignorance of what was going on until the vacuum was destroyed when the extra vehicle was coupled up. No one saw fit to inform the driver. We discovered the nature of the extra vehicle looking back along the train as we went round the curve towards Barnham, where it was again detached.

We left Fareham eight minutes late and from then on our fortunes varied, for we were checked several times by signals, and, as on the outward trip, the Bedhampton p.w. slack was scrupulously observed.

The fire got more and more dirty and clinkered and the coal dust got less and less like coal. Bolingbroke worked continuously with fire irons and shovel, but it was seldom possible to use full regulator and there was seldom more than 150 lb. of steam on the gauge.   So half regulator and 35-30 per cent cut-off were now the order of the day. The extraordinary thing is that speed along the gently undulating track from Farlington Junction to Worthing was generally much higher on this journey than it had been going outwards with good coal, plenty of steam and the same load. It was almost as if the engine ran more freely with less regulator and a lower pressure.

At Worthing we arrived 12 minutes late, and left 11¼ late. The final leg of the journey was made, as far as Southwick, with half regulator, 30 per cent cut-off and 150 lb. of steam. But for the final four miles up at 1 in 242 Wood opened up to full regulator and 35 per cent., and the pressure dropped to 140 lb. but no further. So we ended up at Brighton only 8 minutes late, having won back three minutes in the last 10½ miles.

Checks by signals and the Bedhampton slack, to say nothing of the Fareham delay, more than accounted for time lost. Overall, I give the Brighton Atlantic a nett gain of 3 minutes on schedule. It had been very hard work but a very gallant effort on a regular service duty by a 40+ year-old engine and her Brighton crew.

(The origins of this article are unknown. -Ed)

STRANGERS ON THE SOUTHERN: *Above - Inter-regional working just south of Shawford. In the distance is the private 'Bowkers footbridge'. The fogman's hut on the up side will be noted - although the signals are 'stop' arms.*
Below - No 7818 Granville Manor approaching Romsey with a Southampton Terminus to Cheltenham working.

Both Henry Meyer

Railways may be a professional occupation or a hobby interest but we must never forget they can also result in tragedy. Little details are known of the origins of this situation, the image for which has been recreated and posed for the photographer. We may assume a passenger was leaning out too far and either stuck or was struck by another object - fixed or moving - it matters not. The human body simply cannot withstand such trauma. It was taken on 27 October 1960.

THE LIGHTER SIDE

Motive Power shortage at Bournemouth Central, 4 July 1953?

Human power, in the form of the Platform Inspector, Station Announcer and four porters, pushing a van from east to west along the platform - reported as just passing the Refreshment Room!.

E Knowlman

BEVOIS PARK SIDINGS
- an interlude beside the River Itchen

Peter Tatlow

The author trained and worked as a civil engineer on British Railways, Southern Region from 1957 to 1968 and all photographs are by him.

Within a few months of joining the New Works Drawing Office at Waterloo of the Chief Civil Engineer's Department of the Southern Region in late 1957 as a draughtsman, an interesting project came up which required several site visits to Bevois Park Sidings. These were situated on the up-side of the main line from London, between Mount Pleasant level crossing, Northam and St Denys station on the outskirts of Southampton, whilst on the other side of the line was the River Itchen. The sidings were used as a small marshalling yard to receive, shunt and despatch goods trains to and from the Docks, together with the branch from Fawley, etc.

Adjacent to the railway boundary on the west side were a number of small industrial units. British Railways were keen to develop a substantial area of spare ground between the sidings and the boundary as further units with rail connection, in the hope of gaining traffic thereby. To do so, however, the infrastructure needed to be in place and my part was to design a surface and foul water drainage system.

The first step in any project of this nature was to obtain the 40 foot to one inch survey of the area, of which the railway maintained a reasonably up to date collection in the Plan Arch below Waterloo station. In this case it consisted of a long linen backed cartridge-paper roll, drawn in ink with tinted features, together with a linen tracing from which dye-line prints, or copy negatives could be made. This showed the whole of the line from north of St Denys, the junction with the Netley line, the said Bevois Park sidings, the Mount Pleasant level crossing, further sidings beyond and down to Northam Junction, where the line to Southampton Central station, Bournemouth and Weymouth swung sharply away to the right from the straighter route to Southampton Terminus station. The limitation of the width of the tracing meant, however, that the full extent of the sidings was too wide for it and the end portion of the sidings were drawn elsewhere on the linen where space permitted.

To consider adequately the layout of the proposed development meant, however, it was necessary to prepare a plan of the area under consideration as one whole. During the section engineer John Lambert's absence on leave one week, I embarked on tracing in Indian ink the two necessary halves on to a 40-inch wide piece of tracing linen, only to discover on his return that he had already made a 'gold' copy of the bulk of the yard with sufficient room along one edge to simply trace on the remaining smaller missing portion.

So much for the plan, but the design of a drainage system required consideration of levels as well and the 40 foot survey had none. Another draughtsman and I were therefore detailed to make a site visit to carry out some levelling over the site with a dumpy level and find a suitable outfall for the run-off. Once set up, by looking through the telescope of the level, one could read off on the graduated staff the distance of ground below the horizontal projected by the hair line. Thus by comparing the relative height of various spots on the site, their difference in height could be established against either a temporary bench mark, or preferably a local Ordnance bench mark, the latter often to be found on a masonry building such as a church, or a bridge abutment.

In those days, to make rail journeys on business, senior staff were each issued with a named 'all stations' free pass, probably first class, while lesser mortals went and saw the Chief Clerk the day before and would either be loaned an un-named second class 'all stations' pass, or he would write out and sign a free ticket for the specific journey. If you were lucky enough, or perhaps not, to be travelling with a senior member of staff entitled to first class travel, then yours too would be first class, the intention being that you could discuss the job with him during the journey. Again, if you were out of the office for a sufficient period of time to necessitate a meal, you were entitled on your return to claim expenses of, I think, 6s 6d for lunch, but raised to 8s 6d, if in the company of a senior member of staff.

At the time I lived in Horsley on the New Guildford line, while my colleague had to come down from London, so we agreed that on Wednesday 18 June 1958 I would join the train at Woking and we would travel together to Southampton Central and then back to St Denys, from

Opposite - Original Bulleid No. 34047 Callington passes under Dukes Road bridge as it comes off the line from Fareham and runs beside the banks of the River Itchen on its way to Southampton Central with the daily Brighton to Plymouth through train via Salisbury on 18 June 1958. Note the magnificent four-doll double bracket lattice signal for Up trains approaching the junction.

Above - *Ivatt 2-6-2T Class 2 No 41317, recently overhauled and repainted at Eastleigh Works, pauses in one of the head shunts at Bevois Park during its running-in turn on 23 June 1958 before return to its home depot of Plymouth Friary, transferred to the Western Region earlier in the year.*

Left - *The fireman rests in the cab of Maunsell 0-6-0 Q Class No 30531, which has just arrived on the reception line of Bevois Park Yard on 23 June 1958.*

Later the same day another fireman leans against the cab-side of Urie 4-6-0 H15 class No. 30488 with bogie tender, before setting off to Basingstoke with a goods train.

where it was only a short walk beside the track to the site.

Upon arrival, we made ourselves known to the yard inspector, but, as we were not expecting to work on the main line, had made no arrangements for a lookout-man to be available from the local permanent way gang. Some time was taken reconnoitring the site and a start was made on levelling. Lunch break offered the opportunity to cross the main lines, sit beside the River Itchen and photograph the succession of trains that passed on their way to and from Southampton and further afield, or which stopped in the yard to drop off and pick up wagons or whole trains. At the end of the session, we made our way back to St Denys station from where we caught the diesel set back by the alternative route of Alton, via Winchester; thence by electric on to Aldershot and as in my case change, round via Ash Vale and Ash to Guildford.

What a variety of trains and locomotives passed Bevois Park. As well as the regular timetabled fast and semi fast services from Waterloo to Southampton, Bournemouth

and Weymouth, including the *Bournemouth Belle*; there were the Ocean Liner specials, such as the *Cunarder, The Springbok* and *The Orcadian*, to the ships moored alongside the various quays at Southampton, also the once-a-day through train in each direction between Plymouth and Brighton, via Havant, Southampton, Salisbury, Exeter and Okehampton. Not all local trains had yet been taken over by the diesel multiple units, so a few motor-fitted trains were still to be seen, while running-in trips by freshly painted locomotives just out-shopped from Eastleigh Works were to be encountered.

As well as the occasional parcels train, on the freight side there were the through trains of steam-heated fitted vans loaded with imported bananas or insulated containers for meat. What a sight a long empty container train made as it rattled through St Denys on its way back to the Docks behind a Urie 4-6-0 H15 class, having maintained momentum and clear signals as it ran down from the summit of the line at Litchfield Tunnel. Other more local trip trains

Maunsell 4-4-0 Schools class No. 30903 Charterhouse *heads up the main line with a slow train from Bournemouth on 18 June 1958. Note the 08 class diesel shunter in the background.*

would make their way up from the various quaysides and warehouses, or the Fawley branch and called into Bevois Park Sidings to be re-marshalled and continue their journey to the rest of the country.

Motive power for express passenger work could be any locomotive allocated the Western Division of the Southern Region, including Bulleid 'Merchant Navys' and 'West Country' / 'Battle of Britain' 4-6-2s, a few in their new rebuilt form; 'King Arthurs', H15s and the occasional Lord Nelson 4-6-0s; plus Schools 4-4-0 classes. On the freight side there were S15s and again H15s, Qs, and the odd Maunsell U; BR 4MT 2-6-0s, 3MT 2-6-2Ts, ex-LMS 2MT 2-6-2Ts; Drummond T9s, M7s and 700s working out their time, would undertake the work. Ex-GW Collett 2251 class 0-6-0s were generally to be found on the Didcot to Southampton Terminus trains via Newbury and Winchester, although on one occasion on the way home we caught a glimpse of the restored *City of Truro*, as it passed Shawford.

With the levelling exercise incomplete, further trips were made on the Monday and Friday the next week and

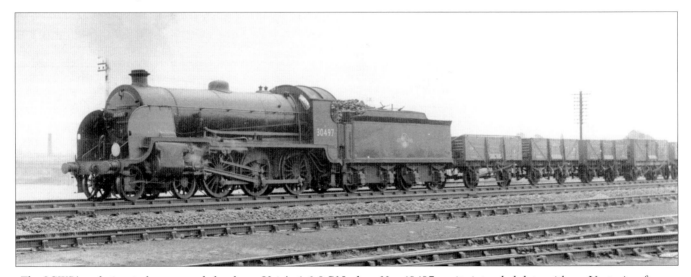

The LSWR's solution to heavy goods haulage, Urie's 4-6-0 S15 class No. 40497 on its intended duty with an Up train of open wagons passes by the banks of the River Itchen on 23 June 1958.

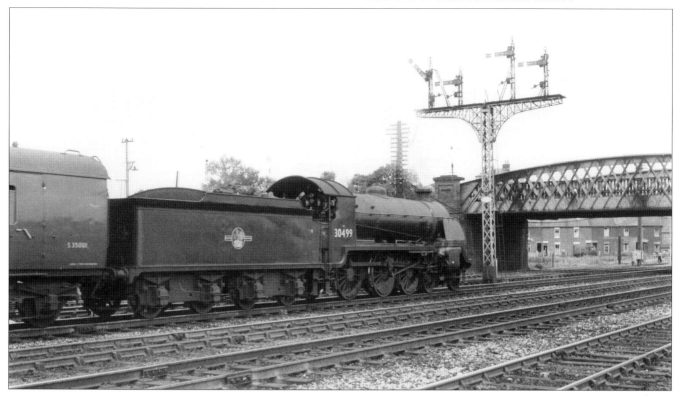

Sister S15 class No. 30499 just as 'at home' on an Up boat train from the Docks to Waterloo on 18 June 1958.

another a week later, ending up with our taking a long set of levels down nearby Imperial Road. This was done firstly to find an appropriate manhole, into which it was hoped the local drainage authority might permit a connection and secondly to tie in with the nearest Ordnance bench mark. These additional days beside the Itchen provided further opportunity to take photographs, on the last occasion extending down to Mount Peasant Crossing with a packed

lunch taken near Northam Junction.

The Hampshire two-car diesel-electric multiple units had just been introduced, displacing many of the 0-4-4T M7 class locomotives fitted for 'push-pull' working. On our return journeys, having ascended the steep gradients of the Hampshire Alps between Winchester and Alton without undue strain, I recall how impressed we were by the speed of these sets on the downhill section beyond

The fireman looks out as Drummond 0-4-4T M7 class No. 30328, not yet ousted by diesel-electric multiple units, pushes a motor set between St Denys and Northam on 23 June 1958.

Over lunch break on 27 June 1958, Merchant Navy class No. 35022 Holland-America Line *gathers pace with a train for Waterloo as it passes Mount Pleasant Crossing between Northam and St Denys.*

Medstead. Having assumed (incorrectly as it transpired) the usual 60-foot long rails and counting the joints, we calculated we were going at over 90 mph, which seemed incredible. Even if they had been 45 foot rails, the low 70s was good going, that is until on our return to the office someone pointed out that during the war the Americans had sent over some 39 foot-long rails, which would have produced a speed of a little under 60 mph!

In the end the Bevois Park scheme came to nothing. The ongoing consequences of the 1955 national rail strike and other economic and practical considerations meant that road transport was rapidly gaining the upper hand and anything less than the transport of bulk commodities was never going to justify traders investing in facilities derived from the use of private sidings and in single wagons loads. The sidings are of course now long closed and the site occupied by various industries including a ready-mix concrete works, none of which contributes to the railway's revenue, other than perhaps some ground rent or the sale of the freehold. Slightly south and on the opposite side of the line, the former sidings at Northam, however, were redeveloped in 2002 as South-West Trains' Train-care facility as the home depot for the Desiro fleet.

Opposite top - *In mid-afternoon BR Standard 2-6-2T No. 82015 and another draw into Bevois Park Sidings with a train of vans from the Docks for marshalling and onward despatch to their various destinations on 3 July 1958.*

Opposite bottom - *Bulleid 4-6-2 West Country class No. 34039* Boscastle *heads the Brighton to Plymouth under the footbridge at Mount Pleasant level crossing on 3 July 1958.*

A grubby Urie mixed traffic 4-6-0 H15 class No. 30482 fulfilling its passenger role with a Down train for Bournemouth as it approaches Northam Junction on 27 July 1958.

Still in the Southampton area...

Stranger on the shore, an unidentified Riddles 2-8-0 at Woolston with the 2.58 pm all stations Southampton Central to Portsmouth train on an unreported date. This is believed to have been the only time an engine of this type worked a passenger service in the Southampton area.
G R Wheeler

Above - Electric Motor Luggage Van No S68002 at Dover in 1960. Introduced in 1959 in connection with the Kent Coast Electrification, the ten vehicles built were to provide additional luggage accommodation primarily on boat train services to Dover and Folkestone. Luggage accommodation was curtailed on these services following the introduction of the fixed-formation electric CEP units which had ousted locomotive hauled trains on this route. Apart from working with the CEP sets, resulting often in a 13-coach train, the vehicles could (if required) operate under their own power on the 3rd-rail network, whilst they also had the bonus of being fitted with batteries for limited use on non-electrified lines - as seen here. Battery use though was limited to around 20-30 minutes. The actual design was based upon a single prototype used as a parcels car on the Tyneside DC network. The bland front end design was also used as the basis for the Southern DEMU and EMU fleet from the late 1950s into the early 1960s. The Tyneside prototype, No 68000, lasted until 1967. The southern variants, 68001-10, were in service until 1991/2 after which they were transferred to departmental duties often as depot shunters. All had been withdrawn by 2004 but nine of the ten were initially preserved, No 68006 withdrawn in 1994 following accident damage at Ramsgate whilst the former 68007 was initially preserved but subsequently scrapped.

Overleaf - Former LSWR 'Ironclad' pantry brake-first No 7714 (the number appears on the coach end) as converted in September 1944 to an inspection car for WD use, numbered WD1647. This was one of two such coaches altered to run as part of an ambulance train. Four were built, LSWR Nos 4061-64, in 1922 for Southampton Docks boat trains and included three compartments for passengers together with a small kitchen and pantry for serving meals (or more probably snacks) on the journey between Waterloo and Southampton. Their SR numbers were 7711-14 and this one, along with No 7711 was converted for War Department use. The others, Nos 7712/13 had been requisitioned by the military at the same time, but as these received somewhat different WD numbers they were probably put to other uses. On their return to the Southern Railway they were again put on boat train services but without the kitchen areas being staffed until 1949, when they were rebuilt as six compartment brake firsts, again remaining on Southampton boat trains until withdrawn in 1958/9. Livery during WD ownership - maybe khaki or grey? (Notes by Mike King)

INSPECTION COACH

TARE
TONS
39

OVERALL LENGTH
& WIDTH
60 FT. 7 INS.
X
9 FT. 3 INS.

4

S.R. 7714

The last new-build locomotive to be completed at Brighton prior to the grouping. No 333 in 1922; named 'Remembrance' in memory of the LB&SCR staff who had given their lives in the World War.

Urie N15 No 749, 'Iseult' in photographic grey and with the later addition of smoke defectors.

THE SOUTHERN RAILWAY FROM INCEPTION TO NATIONALISATION AND BEYOND

Part 5 - Changing Times

Tony Goodyear

The completion of the electrification (and re-electrification) works described in parts 3 and 4 formed what was once portrayed by the "Railway Gazette" as the conclusion of the Southern's electrification schemes. As most of you will know, this was not the case, it was merely a pause for breath. In this instalment we will look at the Southern's efforts to update itself in other areas, while also progressing the less glamorous add-on electrification schemes, and all this is set against a steadily declining economic situation. First though, I must wind the clock back and look at the developments that were taking place during the mid to late 1920s in other areas of the Southern's activities that have so far been neglected. Many of these developments were subtly vital to the success of the early Southern electrification schemes, as well as those that were still but a pipe dream.

When Maunsell took up his new appointment as Chief Mechanical Engineer, it must have been clear to him that the company's priority for investment would be electrification. It therefore followed, with Walker's declared intention to carry out the electrification of the London suburban area, roughly in line with the various constituent companies' previously announced proposals, that any new steam locomotive construction would only be authorised against identified requirements, be that replacement or service improvement. In the case of secondary services they would have to make do with whatever hand-me-down (cascaded) or other locomotives that were made available.

As with the rolling stock building plans put in place by the constituent companies (see Part 4 SW 17 p 99), orders for locomotives were allowed to continue. These included the completion of orders at Ashford, Brighton and Eastleigh. At Ashford works just three N class and one N1 class from the second batch of 15 locomotives remained to be completed. The last new-build locomotive to be completed at Brighton was 4-6-4T No. 333 in 1922; it was

named *Remembrance* in memory of the LB&SCR staff who gave their lives in the First World War, but there was also an order for 12 B4X class 4-4-0s. They were officially classed as rebuilds but, as was often the case, little apart from the bogies and tender frames of the locos they replaced was incorporated into the new locomotives. Just two engines had been completed by the end of 1922, the remainder being built during 1923 with one lingering on into 1924. Many of these engines were released to traffic in grey livery as the new livery for the Southern Railway had yet to be approved. Eastleigh had three Urie N15 class 4-6-0s from the second batch of ten outstanding at the grouping and these locomotives were subsequently incorporated into the 'King Arthur' class. They were given names of people and places associated with the legend, rather than names of Knights of the Round Table, which were bestowed on the later Maunsell 'Arthurs'.

During the latter part of its existence the SE&CR was watching developments at Woolwich Arsenal (see Part 2: SW 8, p77) with the production of 100 N class locomotives ordered by the Government, in two batches of 50 in 1919 (the second batch was in lieu of a similar number of cancelled ROD 2-8-0s). The aim was to reduce unemployment during the rundown of arms production at the munitions works, with the intention of selling the locomotives to the newly nationalised railways. In the event the railways were not nationalised but grouped together into four large groups, thus scuppering the idea. Initially both the SE&CR and the GER had shown some interest in the locomotives but, as matters dragged on with little likelihood of a swift conclusion and the grouping fast approaching, both companies abandoned further negotiations.

With the obvious success of the prototype locomotive No. 810 and the 14 production locomotives Nos. 811-825 (No. 822 was built as a 3 cylinder N1), all having been built at Ashford between June 1920 and the end of 1923, it was clear that the Southern, in particular, would be

Previous instalments in this new insight into the Southern have appeared in issues, 6, 8 13 and 17.

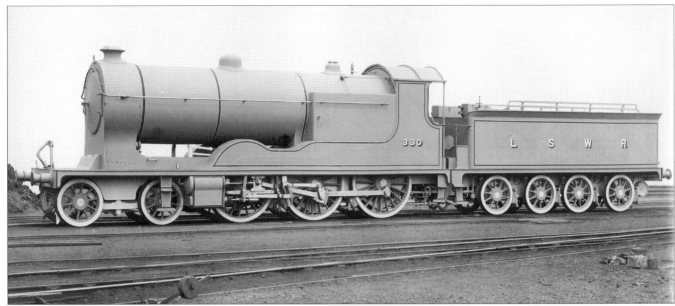

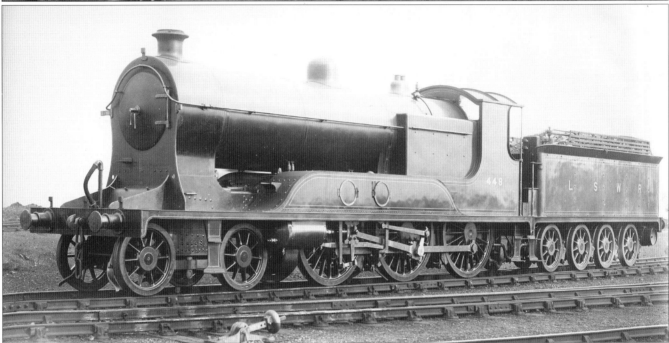

Survivor and not. Top - Drummond F13 4-6-0 No 330 which was rebuilt as an H15 4-6-0 at the end of 1924. Below - P14 No 449 survived for trials and development until 1927, still the last of its class, but was then condemned.

keen to pick up some cheap locomotives of an already tried and tested design. I cannot believe that Sir Herbert Walker, with the contacts he made through his role as acting chairman of the Railway Executive Committee, was not instrumental in facilitating the purchase of 50 sets of N class parts from Woolwich, including boilers built by outside contractors, by the Southern Railway during 1924. There were three distinct purchases of what became SR Locomotives: SR Nos. 826-845 in April (20 sets of parts including partly completed locos), SR Nos. 846-865 in October (20 sets of parts) and Nos. 866-875 in December

(ten sets of parts). Some of the first batch had been partly assembled at Woolwich and at least one locomotive was said to have been trial-steamed. The official completion dates also support the view that many of the first twenty were completed before the second batch of twenty were purchased, there being a three month gap between 845 and 846 entering traffic. For the record, a further 33 sets of parts were disposed of as follows: Midland and Great Western Railway of Ireland; 12 sets of parts: the Great Southern Railway of Ireland (which had absorbed the M & GWR in 1925); 15 sets of parts (one set used as spares and six locos had 6ft driving wheels): and the Metropolitan Railway; six sets of parts, assembled as 2-6-4 tank engines by Armstrong Whitworth & Co. Most of the remaining 17 sets of parts ended up with the Southern, though at least a few extra spares found their way to Ireland.

The Ns were truly Southern Engines having been seen on all three divisions even before the first of the Woolwich batches appeared, by virtue of them being used on services between Tonbridge, Redhill and Reading. A large allocation of Woolwich engines was soon established at Exmouth Junction, for use on main line services to Ilfracombe and Plymouth. The West Country Ns also effectively displaced many of the old Beattie-designed (both Snr. & Jnr.) 0-6-0, 4-4-0 and 4-4-2T locomotives then operating many of the secondary duties on the North Cornwall lines. The 50 cheap, modern, N class locos were most welcome and helped with the urgent replacement of old and worn out engines, thereby avoiding the need for expensive overhauls occupying valuable workshop space; or having to build or buy additional new mixed-traffic locomotives from outside contractors.

However, the Southern's operating authorities had bigger fish to fry as they were already pushing for locomotives capable of handling loads of 500 tons at 55 mph. on the Western Section. As several years would be required to develop and test an entirely new design of locomotive, Maunsell was given authority to develop the existing Urie N15 4-6-0s with a view to further construction. Maunsell's approach to improving the performance of N15s was to redesign the front end (the design team at Ashford modified the layout along the lines of the N class), with streamlined steam passages, smaller cylinders, longer valve travel, outside steam pipes and other minor changes. As luck had it there were outstanding orders placed by the L&SWR for the reconstruction of the 15 Drummond 4-cylinder 4-6-0s of classes F13, P14 and G14 as Urie 2-cylinder H15 4-6-0s. Maunsell had the order for the P14s and G14s changed to the upgraded N15 design but retaining the water cart tenders and bogies from the originals, together with Urie style cabs. Most of the locos were released to traffic between February and July 1925, in time for the 1925 summer timetable. P14s Nos. 448/450-452 and G14s Nos. 453-457 were officially withdrawn in January 1925, the exception being No. 449, which was retained as a trials and development engine, and given a superheated boiler with an extended smokebox. The original 449, having donated its tender, continued as E0449 on the duplicate list until 17 September 1927.

The five F13s Nos. 330-334 were reconstructed as H15s towards the end of 1924 , along the lines of No. 335 which had been dealt with 10 years before in December 1914, all five being back in traffic by the end of January 1925. In addition there was an outstanding order for ten new H15s, Nos. 473-478 and Nos. 521-524, to be constructed at Eastleigh. These locos were delivered between February and September 1924, many parts for them

being fabricated at Ashford. The delivery of five reconstructed and ten newly-constructed engines effectively provided 15 additional H15s available for traffic by the end of January 1925, with some being available for the start of the 1924 summer timetable. With five H15s and ten N15s being officially considered as rebuilds, the cost would most likely have been charged as an operating expense in the accounts. The re-use of the original numbers of the locomotives they directly replaced reinforces this view.

Even before the ten reconstructed N15s took to the road, the Southern authorities were seeking tenders from outside contractors for a further 20 new N15s, to be built to the new Southern composite loading gauge developed by the design team at Ashford, which gave maximum route availability, enabling the locomotives to work over most main line routes on all three sections of the Southern Railway. These powerful engines were urgently required by the operating authorities to handle the anticipated increased loads of the 1925 summer timetable, particularly on the Kent coast services. An order for twenty new N15s, with the modified front end and Ashford pattern cabs, was placed with the North British Locomotive Company during December 1924. Such was the need that the order was subsequently increased by a further ten locomotives at the same price. The first six new locomotives arrived in May 1925, an impressive effort by NBL, by which time the first five of the Eastleigh reconstructed locos were also available for traffic.

Initially the NBL locomotives (known as 'Scotchmen' to railwaymen) were unsatisfactory in service. After a series of trials, followed by changes in driving practices, had produced only limited success, they were called into Eastleigh works for attention to the boilers, axle-boxes and brick arches. On completion of this remedial work, which in some cases almost amounted to an intermediate repair, they reached their full potential and went on to enjoy long and useful careers. Further batches of N15s, built to the composite loading gauge and totalling twenty-five engines in all, were ordered from Eastleigh works during 1925/6. In the event only fourteen locomotives were built, becoming Nos. 793–806, and they ended up with the 3,500 gallon Ashford pattern six-wheel tenders originally specified for the cancelled Nos. 808–817, rather than the 4,000 gallon ones originally proposed for these engines. The locos were blighted in their later careers as the draw-gear on the Ashford pattern tenders was incompatible with that on the Urie tenders fitted to other members of the class, thus limiting their usefulness as substitutes or for cascading elsewhere. The remaining eleven N15 locomotives on order Nos. 807 and 808-817 were changed to 'Lord Nelsons' Nos. 850-860.

Chronologically the next new locomotives to arrive were the first four of the nine K class 2-6-4 tanks Nos. 791-799 erected by Armstrong Whitworth, during May and June 1925, using NBL boilers obtained from Woolwich Arsenal. The first four were received by the end of May. These

Similar in appearance to the L1 class of 1926 were the earlier D1 and E1 types. Here D1 No 31735 is seen at Southampton Terminus with a Salisbury to Portsmouth Harbour parcels working on 4 February 1961.
J C Haydon

engines had a shorter coupled wheelbase than the Ns and hence the parts for the twenty frames required were new, and produced by Ashford works, one set of parts being retained at Ashford and assembled as the solitary 3 cylinder K1 No. 890 at the end of 1925. The remaining ten sets of parts were sent to Brighton works and subsequently appeared between July and December 1926 as Nos. 800-809.

A completely new class of locomotive appeared during the spring of 1926. The new locomotives were known as L1s or, in some circles modified Ls. They were very much a stop gap measure: had Maunsell been quicker off the mark they would have had more in common with the E1 and D1 rebuilds than the Ls. In order to get these locomotives into traffic quickly, the usual expediency of using an existing outstanding order was resorted to. As Ashford could not undertake the work in the timescale required, the fifteen locomotives were ordered from the North British Locomotive Company. In service they were quite capable of working the 300 ton Charing Cross – Folkestone boat trains for which they were intended and they performed well enough, but they lacked the sparkle of the E1 and D1 rebuilds, due to not having the benefit of a modified front end.

The next new locomotive to appear was the first of the 'Lord Nelson' class, No. 850 *Lord Nelson* which entered traffic during August 1926. As with most new designs produced by Maunsell it was thoroughly tested before series production commenced and it was to be May 1928 before No. 851 eventually appeared. The first ten production locomotives took a year to complete, the last being delivered by April 1929. Five more Lord Nelsons were constructed between September and November 1929 and these turned

out to be the last of the class. Originally intended to be part of a larger order for ten Lord Nelsons and fifteen of the new 'Schools' class, the order was subsequently changed to five 'Nelsons', ten 'Schools' and fifteen U1s.

General freight traffic was still on the increase in the mid 1920s, when the first two batches of Maunsell modified S15s were ordered. By the time they were built at Eastleigh during 1927 and early 1928, the signs of a slowdown in the economy were beginning to show. Nonetheless, the first ten were quickly deployed on the western section, with the locomotives equally divided between Salisbury and Exmouth Junction sheds, the second batch of five going straight to Feltham.

The first U class locomotive to appear in traffic was No. 805 in March 1928, having been rebuilt from a K class 2-6-4T ('River' class) that had originally been new in October 1926, just eighteen months before. The obvious reasons for converting the twenty 2-6-4 tanks are well known, but there were also other factors, apart from the direct consequences of the Sevenoaks crash, that must have been taken into account by Sir Herbert Walker when he ordered the rebuilding of all of the 'River' class tanks as 2-6-0 tender locos. The Sevenoaks crash was officially put down to the poor state of the track following heavy rain and the tendency of these engines to roll from side to side at speed on poor track. This was exacerbated by the water sloshing around in the side tanks as a result of the high centre of gravity and the lack of tank baffles. It should also be remembered that these locomotives had been involved in a number of previous incidents. When Walker made his decision to rebuild the whole class he would have taken all these factors into consideration, along with the views of the staff involved with the operation and working of the

A pair of Z class 0-8-0Ts, Nos 30952 and 30957 take a break from banking duties at Exeter Central in August 1959. Horace H Bleads

locomotives. He also had to be seen to take into account the recommendations of Sir Nigel Gresley, following test running of the locomotives on the Great Northern and Western section main lines. Other issues also emerged as part of the enquiries into what happened. Operators and enginemen considered that a tender engine would be more stable on the Eastern section's somewhat indifferent track. It is also well documented that there were issues with the engines having insufficient water capacity to get from London to Dover safely on just one full tank of water, resulting in some diagrams being deemed unsuitable and others having station stops extended specifically to top up the tanks. The conversion to tender locomotives almost doubled the water capacity available, which increased both operational flexibility and the effective range of the locomotives.

After conversion to a 2-6-0, No. 805 was subjected to trials and test running. It was to be a further three months before the main rebuild programme kicked in with all three works taking on a share of the conversion work. Eighteen further locomotives were completed between June and August 1928. However, the repairs and conversion of No. 800, the Sevenoaks victim, were not completed until the December. Concurrently with the 'River' class rebuilding programme, delivery of the first of the new batch of U class locomotives proper (previously ordered as 2-6-4T) was getting underway from Brighton works. The first, No. 613, was released to traffic in June 1928 along with converted engines Nos. 803/804/806 & 807. A second batch of ten engines appeared from Ashford, numbered 620-629, between November 1928 and December 1929. These engines were easily distinguishable from the converted

engines, having a much higher running plate, rather accentuating the height of the 6ft. driving wheels. The solitary K1 3-cylinder 2-6-4T No. 890 was converted at Ashford works in June 1928, complete with its conjugated valve gear, and thus became the first U1 class locomotive.

During 1929 eight rather ungainly looking 0-8-0 shunting tank engines appeared from Brighton works, officially designated as the Z class but often referred to as "Maggies". The design was a cleverly thought out solution to a problem, in that they were specifically designed for yard and hump shunting; with a large non-superheated parallel boiler and small firebox of a standard Brighton design, which was able to retain heat while idle without blowing off excessively. Originally they were intended to be used for transfer work as well, but without pony wheels (proposed but not pursued) they had a distinct waddle, even at slow speed, and were little used in this role. In later life they were used very successfully as bankers at Exeter, and occasionally elsewhere. An order for a further ten was cancelled due the economic downturn, the next order for shunting locos being for diesels.

The first ten of Maunsell's 3-cylinder 'Schools' class 4-4-0s were built at Eastleigh between March and July 1930. Universally accepted as Maunsell's masterpiece, they were, in fact, a bit of a compromise, the original intention being to produce a shortened version of a 'Lord Nelson'. As is often the case things didn't quite go according to plan. The original brief was for an engine that could haul loads up to 400 tons at an average speed of 55 mph. and work over certain weight-restricted routes. Maunsell's preferred design used a shortened version of the 'Nelson' boiler with Belpaire firebox, three cylinders and four- coupled wheels.

New & Reconstructed Locomotives Completed By SR between Jan 1923 and 31 May 1925 (for summer timetable), for completeness order and completion dates shown separately,

SE&CR Locos completed by S R				
Class	Original order	Number outstanding on 01/01/1923	Order completed	Notes
N (2-6-0)	15	3	12/1923 All built at Ashford	only 14 built as N class
N1 (2-6-0)	1	1	03/1923 Built at Ashford	15th Loco from N order

LBSCR Locos completed by SR				
B4X (4-4-0)	12	10	Early 1924 All rebuilt at Brighton	

L&SWR Locos completed by SR				
N15 (Urie) (4-6-0)	10 13/10/1921	3 All built at Eastleigh	03/1923	Second batch

SR Built Locos (including reconstructed Locos) 01/01/1923 – 31/12/1925				
Class	Number ordered	Number completed by 31 May 1925	Construction Dates	Notes
N15 (4-6-0)	10 09/1924	6	02/1925 - 07/1925 All built at Eastleigh	Maunsell/Eastleigh Cab Reconstructed G14s & P14s Nos. 448 – 457
N15 (4-6-0)	20 from NBL 17/12/1924 + 10 28/01/1925 + 15 from Eastleigh* 29/05/1925	6 (from NBL) -	05/1925 - 09/1925 NBL 03/1926 - 01/1927 Eastleigh	Maunsell/Ashford Cab NBL Nos. 763 – 782, 783 – 792 Eastleigh Nos. 793 – 806 (only 14 completed)*
H15 (4-6-0) (ex F13)	5 05/1923	5	11/1924 - 01/1925 Eastleigh	Reconstructed F13s Nos. 330 - 334
H15 (4-6-0)	10 05/1923	10	02/1924 - 09/1924 Eastleigh	Maunsell/Eastleigh Cab Nos. 473 – 478, 521 -524
N (2-6-0)	20 sets of parts purchased from Woolwich 04/1924, + 20, 10/1924 + 10, 11/1924, 50 in total	39	05/1924 - 09/1925 All assembled at Ashford	Some locos partially completed at Woolwich but all were completed and made ready for traffic at Ashford. Nos. 826 - 845, 846 - 865, 866 - 875
K (2-6-4T)	9 assembled by Armstrong Whitworth from parts supplied from Ashford and Woolwich. 10 built at Brighton using some parts from Ashford and Woolwich	4	05/1925 – 06/1925 Armstrong Whitworth 07/1926 - 12/1926 Assembled at Brighton	Nos. 791 – 799 Note: Armstrong Whitworth assembled the 6 2-6-4Ts for the Metropolitan Rly from Woolwich parts during 03 & 04/1925 (no coincidence, I suspect, that they were given order as they would be well placed to complete the SR order quickly). Nos. 800 - 809
K1 (2-6-4T)	1 assembled from the remaining set of parts ordered for the K class	1	12/1925 Ashford	No. 890
* Only 14 locos completed as 'King Arthurs' 15th Loco completed as first 'Lord Nelson' No. 850				

SR built locos (including rebuilt engines) 01/01/1926 – 31/12/1930				
Class	Numbers Ordered	Number completed by 31/12/1930	Construction Dates	Notes
L1 (4-4-0)	15 From NBL	15	03/1926 - 05/1926 NBL	Nos. 753 – 759 & 782 - 789
LN (4-6-0)	1 Eastleigh 05/1925 10 Eastleigh 03/1927 5 Eastleigh (added to order above 1928)	16	08/1926 06/1928 - 04/1929 09/1929 - 11/1929	No. 850 Nos. 851 -860 Nos. 861 - 865
S15 (4-6-0)	10 Eastleigh 05/1925 5 Eastleigh 03/1926	10 5	03/1927 – 09/1927 10/1927 – 12/1927	Nos. 823 – 831 Nos. 832 – 837 *Nos. 838 – 847 built 1936*
U (2-6-0) converted from K class 2-6-4 tanks	*7 Eastleigh 1928 7 Ashford 1928 6 Brighton 1928*	*Total 20*	*06/1928 – 07/1928* *03/1928 – 12/1928* *06/1928 – 07/1928*	*Nos. 790 – 796* *Nos. 797 – 802/805* *Nos. 803/804/806 - 809*
U (2-6-0) new build	10 Brighton 10 Ashford	20	10 06/1928 – 12/1928 10 11/1928 – 12/1929	Nos. 610 -619 Nos. 820 - 829 All ordered as 2-6-4Ts, order changed to tender locos following Sevenoaks crash. *Nos. 630 – 639 ordered as 2-6-0s built 1931*
U1 (2-6-0) converted K1 class 2-6-4 tank	*1 Ashford 1928*	*1*	*06/1928*	*No. 890* *New build Nos. 1891 – 1910 ordered as 2-6-0s built 1931*
Z (0-8-0T)	8 Brighton 1928	8	1929	Nos. 950 - 957
V (4-4-0)	10 Eastleigh 1928	10	03/1930 – 07/1930	Nos. 900 – 909 *Nos. 910 -939 built 1932 - 1935*

However, it subsequently transpired that the Eastern section Operating Department also wanted these locos to be able to work over the Hastings line, but the width restrictions imposed on this line precluded the use of a Belpaire boiler due to the impaired forward vision that would result. A shortened version of the excellent `King Arthur' boiler was substituted but with a reduced taper of just 1 inch. In order to pass through the restricted width tunnels on the Hastings line, a new pattern 4,000 gallon tender, with turned-in top to match the angled profile of the cab, was also designed. The first ten locomotives differed from later batches in a number of respects. The most obvious was the construction and appearance of the cab. On the later locomotives, the top line of the side lookouts and the cab windows were higher, and the rain strip on the roof was also altered to suit. The first

batch of locomotives were intended for service on the Hastings line, but the necessary engineering works were incomplete, so six were based at Dover and used on the Dover and Deal services to London for over a year. The other four engines went new to Eastbourne for the London services. Three further batches of ten locomotives each were built between December 1932 and July 1935.

There remains one further locomotive to be mentioned and that was the extra 1ft. 11½ gauge 2-6-2T No.188 *Lew* for the Lynton and Barnstaple Railway, which was ordered from Manning Wardle & Co. and delivered in 1925.

The tables show that only essential and opportunistic steam locomotives continued to be authorised after the grouping. No new branch, small passenger or

Year	Locomotives Built	Year	Locomotives Built
1923	*16**	1927	17
1924	*34 + 1**	1928	19
1925	81	1929	24
1926	38	1930	10
* locomotives or rebuilds ordered pre-grouping shown in italics			

goods engines were approved as there would be a surplus of suitable engines for cascading down to other work following completion of the proposed electrification works. Additionally, a number of previously placed orders were altered to reflect the changed circumstances of the mid to late 1920s e.g. orders for mixed traffic locos were changed to express passenger, and some orders were cancelled altogether. The table also shows that lead times were such that only the existing outstanding orders for 17 new and rebuilt engines were completed during 1923 (with just the one B4X still outstanding at the end of the year). The Southern authorised and built an additional 115 locomotives during the first three years of its existence, including the 50 N class "loco kits" and the changed H15 and N15 orders, with the first of the new build H15s appearing in early 1924. As final table at the top of the page shows, only another 108 locomotives were authorised and completed over the following five years to 31st December 1930.

You may ask why this so significant, but the tables do show the effects of the Southern's investment in electrification on the requirement for new locomotives and also the deteriorating financial conditions, resulting in fewer locomotives being required to maintain services. The late twenties and early thirties saw off large numbers of older locomotives when they required heavy repairs, some only 40 or so years old. Many engines awaiting their fate were stored out use for long periods at strategic points around the system, before the call to the works or scrap man. Eastleigh and Horsted Keynes were well known for their long lines of stored locomotives.

Even though the Southern inherited a largely modern fleet of turbine-driven ships for the cross-Channel services, it was still necessary to order new vessels to make good war losses and provide larger ships to expand capacity and services. Between 1924 and the end of 1930 twenty seven new vessels entered service. These ranged from well known cross-Channel passenger ferries such as the *Maid of Kent* and the *Canterbury*, down to more modest cargo ships and the first of a new breed of drive on/drive off car ferries, the *Fishbourne*, supplied by Denny's in 1927, for the new car ferry service between Portsmouth and Fishbourne on the Isle of Wight. A new slipway and approach road were built at Fishbourne for the service; such was its success that a further vessel the *Wootton* was supplied by Denny's in 1928.

In Part 3 (SW issue 13, p99) I referred briefly to the Southern Railway inheriting a number of on-going projects from its constituent companies: additionally it also devised several small schemes of its own that were particularly intended to unify the operations and staff of the constituent companies, as well as eliminating the additional costs of duplicated operations.

The first of the inherited schemes from the L&SWR in order of opening was the Totton, Hythe & Fawley Light Railway, which ran down the western side of Southampton Water. The L&SWR had originally obtained powers for the line in 1903 but nothing further was done at the time. The scheme was revived in 1921, principally to serve the new Fawley oil refinery which was being built by the Atlantic Gulf and West Indies Company (subsequently acquired by Esso in 1925). An independent company was formed to construct the line, which was officially opened on 20 July 1925 and then transferred to the Southern Railway.

The second scheme (opened just one week later) was the rebuilding and extension of the North Devon & Cornwall Light Railway, which was originally built as the 6½ mile 3ft gauge Torrington & Marland Railway, principally intended for the transport of china clay. The L&SWR had planned to upgrade the line prior to the First World War but the war and subsequent grouping delayed the opening until 27 July 1925. The line itself was converted to standard gauge and extended a further 13½ miles to join the North Cornwall line at Halwill Junction. The original section from Torrington to Marland was operated as a dual gauge section for a short period following the opening through to Halwill.

Another scheme delayed by the war was the rationalisation and unification of the former SER and LCD lines in north-east Thanet. Both companies served the area with totally separate services, on a sort of "never the twain shall meet" basis. The working agreement creating the South Eastern & Chatham Railway Companies Managing Committee (SE&CR), which resulted in the pooling of staff, rolling stock and receipts of the two companies, operated from 1st January 1899. The new organisation subsequently proposed the rationalisation and combining of the two systems, serving the area by building a new line just short of 1½ miles long connecting the two at Ramsgate to form a circular route round the Thanet coast. The new arrangements came into force on 2 July 1926, with the opening of a large new two-island platform station at Ramsgate and a smaller single island platform one at Dumpton Park, together with major improvements at Margate West (later just Margate). The SER stations at

Scenes on the Totton, Hythe & Fawley Light Railway.

Top - *The terminus of the branch at Fawley, M7 No 357 awaiting a return to Totton and Southampton. The roles of the six men were (L to R): Shunter, Porter, Guard, Stationmaster, Driver and Fireman. 13 April 1940.*

Centre - *Marchwood station at 7.01 pm on the same day. This time it is T1 0-4-4T No 8 with the 6.43 pm Fawley to Southampton Terminus working.*

Bottom - *A12 0-4-2 No 628 on the branch goods, recorded near Marchwood in August 1938. (The photographer noted the time as being 5.50 pm 13 April 1940.)*

All R F Roberts courtesy Stephenson Locomotive Society.

Map - *New, and old abandoned lines in Ramsgate, Margate and Broadstairs district 1926.*

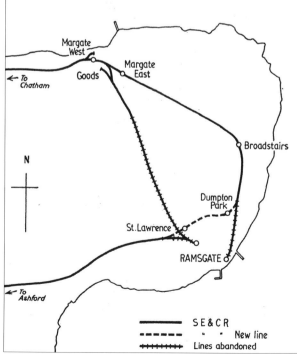

Ramsgate carriage shed (and servicing gantry), 1960. Steve Godden

Margate Sands and Ramsgate Town, together with the LCD station at Ramsgate Harbour were closed. In total, just over five miles of railway were abandoned, with just a short section retained at the Margate end to access the Tivoli goods depot via a new spur. Subsequently, in 1926 a new motive power depot and carriage-cleaning sheds were authorised and built on land immediately to the north of the new Ramsgate station. This work was completed during 1930.

Soon after the formation of the Southern Railway, two proposals to develop transport links in parts of south-west London by the then new London Traffic 'Combine' (an organisation set up to coordinate transport within the London area – a forerunner of the LPTB) caused considerable anguish at Waterloo. Back in 1910 Parliament had sanctioned a new independently-promoted railway to run between Wimbledon and Sutton. As approved, the new railway would have formed an end-on junction with the north side bay platforms at Wimbledon. In the event the scheme foundered, the powers being disposed of to the District railway in 1912 and no further work was carried out prior to the war. In 1923 the new London Traffic 'Combine' proposed to revive this scheme and form a junction with it at Morden by extending the City & South London tube line from Clapham Common to Morden, with

the line continuing to Sutton. Naturally the Southern considered this as an intrusion into its territory and damaging to its interests. Once again we see Walker's abilities as a negotiator put to good use, and, following discussions with his old friend Lord Ashcroft, it was agreed that the Southern would take on the building of the Wimbledon to Sutton line and the City and South London tube line would be extended only as far as Morden, however the physical junction was abandoned as was the opportunity to provide interchange facilities at Morden South. The City and South London tube line extension (today's Northern Line) was opened on 13 September 1926. The Southern chairman in his annual report for 1928 stated that the company had lost 4 million passengers since the opening of the City and South London line. The completion of the Southern's Wimbledon to Sutton line was not achieved until 5 January 1930. However, a short 1¼ mile section as far as South Merton was opened on 7 July 1929 and temporarily worked as a single line beyond Wimbledon 'C' box.

One of the first acts of the new Southern Railway Company was to authorise the provision of openings in the dividing wall between the Brighton and Chatham stations at Victoria. Work commenced in January 1924 (a quick fix!) and the concourse area on the Chatham side was enlarged by shortening one road, eliminating another and realigning the

The old and then new at Exeter Queen Street. Top is the layout and train sheds as existed before the remodelling. Below is subsequent to this, albeit in BR days. No 34038 'Lynton' is leaving for Salisbury and Waterloo on 5 August 1955. The formation of the train is interesting with the three vans nearest the engine. Compared with the earlier view, the scene is neat and functional, the through lines affording access for engine changing when necessary.

buffer stops on the remaining platform lines to match. Subsequently, the platforms in both stations were renumbered, the new No. 1 platform being the most easterly in the old Chatham station.

On 24 June 1924 Sir Herbert Walker gave Dover Corporation details of the Company's proposed improvements in and around Dover, the main purpose of which was to improve Dover Priory station. The first part of the integrated programme of works was the construction of a new motive power depot on partly-reclaimed land to the south of Town station. Work commenced during 1924 and the new depot was opened in 1928, the old LCDR depot at Priory closing at the same time. Harbour station was also demolished and additional yards provided. An additional line of rails was provided through Archcliffe to complete the double track to Hawkesbury Street Junction. Dover Priory Station layout was subsequently remodelled and the platforms extended between 1930 & 1932. A reversible platform loop was provided on the up side, enabling trains to start and finish their journeys clear of the main running lines. A new signal box was provided and commissioned on

16th November 1930, replacing the old LC&DR one. The old LC&DR station buildings were also replaced with new Southern style ones, this part of the improvement scheme being completed in May 1932.

Some schemes didn't even make it to the drawing-board stage; one such was the nominally independent `Southern Heights Light Railway', first proposed in 1925. It was the intention that the Southern would take on the line, which would have run between Orpington to a junction with the Oxted line in the vicinity of Riddlesdown. Some initial planning was done but two issues effectively saw the scheme off; the first being the shaky financial case and the second, the rapidly deteriorating financial climate.

The L&SWR also handed on some long running upgrading and rebuilding schemes in the West Country; significant among these were Exeter, Exmouth, Ilfracombe and Seaton Junction.

By far the most comprehensive of these schemes was the remodelling and rebuilding of Exeter Queen Street station: this was a particularly long drawn out affair originally planned before the grouping, with material

Seaton Junction: old and new. The Southern rebuilding was comprehensive and the Up side station buildings were the only part of the original station to survive. Initial work consisted of constructing a new down platform, together with a separate platform alongside the branch, finally bringing to an end the need to shunt to the branch via the reversing siding. The Down line was diverted on to its new alignment on 13 February 1927 and both the new Down and branch platforms were brought into use, worked from the original signal box. On 3rd April the following year a new L&SWR (type 4A) signal box was brought into use, situated at the country end between the `V' of the Down and branch platforms and contained a new 55-lever Stevens pattern frame. The new Down Through Line was officially brought into use on the 1 April 1928 and the Up Through Line was commissioned on 4 July.

Lower - *The surviving original Tite designed Up side station buildings, the canopy dating from the 1927/8 rebuilding as, U No 31632 passes on an up freight 23 July 1962. Ian Wood.*

ordering and some preparatory work being carried out. The first really tangible evidence of the changes was the opening of a new L&SW (type 4B) signal box with a 35 lever Stevens pattern frame on 13 September 1925, initially known as Exeter Queen Street `C', and later `B', box. Further work on the layout allowed the opening of a second new signal box on 15 June 1927, known as Queen Street `A' (`C' box changed its suffix to `B' at the same time). A 90-lever Stevens pattern frame was provided in what later became known as a type 11A box (very similar to a type 4 but very much updated). Subsequently new station buildings were also provided, in the new Southern style but the

construction was primarily of brick, a little softer on the eye than the later concrete offerings. The new station finally opened as Exeter Central on 1 July 1933, with both signal boxes being renamed at the same time.

In the case of Ilfracombe, the improvements were driven by the need to extend the platforms, in order to eliminate the practice of some passengers from long non-corridor trains having to climb down ladders and walk along the ballast to reach the platform. The original platforms had already been extended in the late 19th century but with a growth in traffic the length of trains using the line had grown again. In the 1920s the Southern approach was more comprehensive as the 42ft turntable also needed to be replaced to handle the larger locomotives now working the line. It was therefore decided to move the entire loco facilities to a new site further to the South; this had the added bonus of allowing a modest improvement in the goods facilities by rearranging the yard. A large quantity of rock was excavated to level the site for the new 65ft turntable. A new single road shed, constructed of concrete blocks with a pitched asbestos roof over one of the roads leading to the turntable was added in 1929. The island platform was extended by approximately 260ft and a new SR (type 11C) signal box was opened on 10 April 1929 containing a 50-lever Westinghouse A2 frame.

At Exmouth, the opening of the branch to Budleigh Salterton in 1903 made the original station somewhat cramped, a problem exacerbated in the summer months as holiday traffic built up. The L&SWR had developed plans to rebuild the station before the grouping but it fell to the Southern to carry out the work. The original single-island platform station disappeared as construction progressed, and an impressive new two-island (4 platform faces) station, in the new Southern style, emerged in its place. The new facilities included a grand two-storey frontage with a large centrally placed clock above. Facilities on the platform side were equally impressive with wide 600ft long platforms, and a glazed concourse with 320ft glazed canopies on each island platform. A new engine shed built from concrete blocks was positioned opposite the end of No. 4 Road. A large new goods shed was also provided in the remodelled yard, together with additional sidings and improved access to the Exmouth Docks branch. The branch was only worked during daylight hours with the locomotive propelling the wagons towards the docks and hauling them on the return journey. A flagman accompanied each train and speed was restricted to 4mph. A large L&SWR (type 4A) signal box with a 70-lever Stevens Pattern frame was erected between the tracks at the station throat, to control the revised layout. One interesting feature was the provision of a balcony on each side of the box to facilitate the exchange of the single line tablets.

The situation at Seaton Junction was quite complex and had existed since the branch to Seaton opened in March 1868. As built the branch could only be accessed via a reversing siding on the down side, no platform being provided on the branch itself, passenger trains then accessing the down platform. This unusual arrangement was commented on in Colonel Yolland's original report to the Board of Trade following his inspection of the Seaton branch on 27 December 1867, Colonel Yolland refused to allow the branch to open until this and many other matters were resolved. In his report Colonel Yolland recommended that a platform should be provided alongside the branch. He re-inspected the works on 19 February 1868; although the platform had not been built he informed the Board of Trade that the branch could be opened, provided an undertaking was given that the branch platform would be built within six

months. In fact it had to wait nearly sixty years until the Southern rebuilt the station in 1927/8, as only a short west-facing bay had been provided, in response to the undertaking given to the Board of Trade: but it still required a shunt move, with passengers, to gain access, though it did have its own canopy.

Moving away now from the western section, and following the completion of the main Eastern section suburban electrification, three further extensions to the existing electrified network were undertaken, all three being introduced on 6 July 1930, adding an additional 24¾ route miles to the electrified network. An obvious extension to the Eastern section electrification was the section of the North Kent line between Dartford and Gravesend, as it was only 7½ miles and 5 station stops from Dartford to Gravesend. Additionally, Swanscombe Halt was rebuilt on a new site and a new substation, with two 1,250kW rotary converters, was provided at Northfleet, which was fed from the existing Lewisham Power and Distribution Control Room. Off-peak train services were provided by extending the existing Charing Cross to Dartford services through to Gravesend with additional services from Cannon Street and other extras added during the peak.

Another useful addition to the electrified network

Durnsford Road 1959. Steve Godden

Waddon Marsh looking east - an undated view. E Wallis.

on the Western section was the Windsor line, where electrification was being extended from Whitton and Hounslow Junctions (the non-electrified two sides of the triangular junction) to Windsor, some 12½ route miles. The work involved the provision of two new stations, at Sheen in the form of an island platform and at Whitton, where the more traditional two-platform approach was adopted; strangely neither of these two stations was on the newly-electrified section. The existing station at Staines was also considerably altered, with extended platforms and new buildings on the downside. The upside buildings were altered at the same time. New substations were provided at Ashford and Datchet; both were supplied from the existing Durnsford Road power house and fitted with two 1,250kW rotary converters.

The third electrification scheme was very much an infill between existing electrified sections: the line between Wimbledon and West Croydon connected with the already electrified lines at each end and in the middle at Mitcham Junction, adding just over 6 miles to the electrified total. Unusually for an electrified line, most of it was single track with short sections of double track between Wimbledon & Merton Park (950yds.), Mitcham & Mitcham Junction

(660yds) and a new passing loop together with a new island platform station and signal box at Waddon Marsh. The three single line sections: Merton Park to Mitcham, Mitcham Junction to Waddon Marsh and Waddon Marsh to West Croydon were all controlled by full size Electric Train Staff instruments. A second non-electrified running line controlled by Miniature Electric Train Staff instruments was provided between Waddon Marsh and West Croydon, solely for the goods traffic to the gas works and the many other rail-connected sites which stretched out alongside a long siding almost as far as Beddington Lane Crossing. In this case the power for the third rail was fed in from each end and the middle from the nearest existing substation.

The extra rolling stock required for the Gravesend and Windsor schemes was catered for as part of the ongoing steam stock conversion programme, which was still delivering small numbers of additional 3-SUB units during the 1930s. The rolling stock solution for the Wimbledon to West Croydon line was very different to the standard 3-SUB option. In part 4 (SW17, p98) reference was made to the rebuilding of the South London Line driving trailers (converted from LB&SCR steam stock when the original South London sets were reduced to two cars) being rebuilt as part of the 3-SUB conversion programme. The fate of all the original SL stock is bound up in the creation of twelve two-car electric units. The first eight two-car units were built from the sixteen original South London Motor Brake Thirds. All the original AC electrical equipment was stripped out, and the vehicles were then rebuilt, eight as Driving Motor Brake Thirds and eight as Driving Trailer Composites. These vehicles retained most of their original open side corridor layout as part of the rebuild, with just the DTCs having two bays converted into compartments for first class passengers. The units were designated 2-SL Nos.

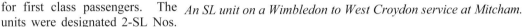

An SL unit on a Wimbledon to West Croydon service at Mitcham.

1901-1908 and were sent back to their old haunts on the South London, always recognisable by their flat roof at the front of each car (left over from where the pantograph used to be). For the Wimbledon – West Croydon services four more two-car units were created, but this time they were rebuilt from the eight South London Trailer First's removed from the original SL sets between 1910 and 1912 and then used as steam hauled stock. These vehicles were taken into works and reappeared as four Driving Motor Brake Composites and four Driving Trailer Thirds, again with open side corridors, including first class, the intention being to use a conductor guard on these services. The units were designated 2-WIM, numbered 1909-1912 and spent most of their lives trundling back and forth between Wimbledon and West Croydon. It was rare to see either of these two types away from their designated services, but it did happen occasionally with the odd WIM unit appearing on the South London and vice versa.

Prior to the grouping, many of the larger railway companies had developed rural bus services; it has to be said mainly as a means of generating additional business for the railway companies, by connecting otherwise isolated rural communities to a suitable railway station. The Great Western was particularly active in this field, having started as early as 1903 with a service between Helston and the Lizard in Cornwall. The L&SWR had also operated bus services between Exeter and Chagford, and from Haslemere to Farnham via Hindhead. The legal position was also far from clear as some pre-grouping railway companies had been granted statutory powers for operating road services, while others had been turned down, the L&SWR and LB&SCR among them. The Railways Act of 1921 made no provision for the operation of road services; the big four railway companies applied to Parliament for such powers

and these were granted on 3 August 1928. In the case of the Southern, the emphasis was to be on investing in the bus companies in their area, rather than entering into direct competition with them, with the object of promoting through ticketing, connecting rail and bus services, joint timetabling and the promotion of rail and road tours. By the end of 1930 the Southern had built up a stake in a number of bus companies: Aldershot & District, Devon General, East Kent, Hants & Dorset, Maidstone & District, Southdown, Southern National, Southern Vectis, Thames Valley and Wilts & Dorset. As part of the process of alternative investment, the big four railway companies also jointly acquired two road transport companies namely: Carter Patterson and Hays Wharf Cartage which included the well known firm of Pickfords.

This article completes the story of the first seven years of the Southern's existence up to 1930(-ish), the not so flying start through the frantic early `20s and onwards into the late `20s/early `30s financial downturn. All the signs of a downturn are there in contemporary writings of the time and in the minutes of the Southern Railway's annual general meetings, clearly showing falling receipts. On this basis the Southern must have been finding it more difficult to fund further investment, so how did they carry out the Brighton line electrification? Logically the next article in this series is Main Line Electrification; the intention is to look at how this was achieved against the financial circumstances of the time and what were the consequences, and maybe unexpected benefits, elsewhere around the system. My thanks go to Martin Stone for checking through the draft copy and correcting the inevitable mistakes, as well as his considerable input in sorting out the several conflicting stories that arose when compiling this article.

THE NARROW GAUGE RAILWAY AT ASHCOTT

(IN THE MYSTERIOUS AND MISTY SOMERSET PEAT FIELDS)

Mike Jacobs

Almost since the dawn of the narrow gauge railway the notion of "portable" track to serve temporary needs has existed. This is particularly true of the 2ft gauge and its near widths, and was greatly endorsed by the use of the extensive systems of narrow gauge lines which were constructed and moved around to serve the Allied war effort during the great war of 1914-1918. These military lines served two historical purposes for existing and subsequent commercial installation; the first was an ample demonstration of the ability of lightly laid lines to deal with the shifting of large tonnages without the need for too many earthworks, and the second was to provide a large legacy of track, locomotives and rolling stock for commercial use once the war ended and their original *raison d'être* disappeared.

Many local systems operated throughout the United Kingdom, serving a wide variety of needs, but, of course, the existence of many was fairly quickly eroded, curiously enough, by other hangovers from the war - the motor lorry and tracked vehicles developed from tank technology. A number of systems had reasonably long lives, especially those that served particular varieties of terrain, but in the two decades after the second war their numbers diminished rapidly.

One of the longer-lived systems operated in the territory served by the Somerset and Dorset Joint Railway, hence this brief article's legitimate inclusion in "Southern Way". The Somerset levels have long been noted for the extraction of sedge peat for agricultural and horticultural purposes, and, in times past, as I can attest from a period of wartime residence in the area as a child, as domestic fuel, albeit of rather low thermal effectiveness. Peat extraction is nowadays, of course, considered to be very environmentally -unfriendly, and does not now occur on its previous enormous scale. Once, however, in common with like regions in the rest of the British Isles, the peat fields in this area covered a huge acreage, served by a network of railways, in this case of 2ft gauge.

One of the major players in peat extraction in this part of Somerset was the long-standing Eclipse Peat Company, a successor to earlier enterprises and itself later owned by Fisons. The railway system which Eclipse Peat operated was developed from 1922, originally using horse traction, but acquiring locomotives from the 1930s onwards. The majority of the locomotives were Lister petrol tractors, some assembled on site from kits, but over the years machines from other manufacturers, such as Muir Hill. Motor Rail and Ruston & Hornsby, appeared, together with

Opposite - Late on a misty October Saturday morning in the depths of the peat fields. A permanent way gang – well, two men – ride their Lister tractor back to the base at Ashcott.
Right - The RCTS "Special" at the end of its run into the furthest reaches of the peat fields. The locomotive is Lister No 25366, and the train consists of three standard peat wagons, slightly cleaned out for the benefit of their human passengers. Note the traditional pyramids of drying peat in the background.

Above - *The unloading bank serving the system to the west of the highway. Road transport carried the peat from here across the highway to the processing plant on the east side.*

Left - *The processing plant was served by the separate railway system on the east side of the highway. Full and empty peat wagons are in the sidings, with an unusual three-way point in the foreground. There is an interesting approach to curves.*

Opposite top - *The driver of Lister No 25366 telephones to seek permission to take his train across the Somerset and Dorset Highbridge branch.*

Opposite bottom - *The EPCL's flat crossing with the Highbridge branch where the 1949 accident took place.*

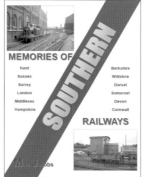

one or two locally created curiosities. The railway system was used to take workers to the points where peat was being extracted and worked with, and to take peat from the fields to the processing plant at Ashcott. For a long time Alexander siding half a mile to the west of Ashcott S&D station provided an interchange for freight between the narrow and the standard gauge, and a little to the east of this was one of the narrow gauge's claims to fame - a flat crossing with the S&D which operated quietly for years, but which caused temporary consternation in 1949 when a standard gauge train from Highbridge collided with one of the Listers.

On the foggy morning of 29 August 1949 (and even in the summer fogs are endemic in these parts) the Lister, with two peat wagons in tow, stalled on the crossing. The driver attempted to uncouple the trucks and move the locomotive, but to no avail. He then ran down the track in an effort to halt the approaching standard gauge mixed train, but the fog rendered him invisible to the crew of 3F 0-6-0 3260 (ex-S&D 76), which collided with the EPCL train and was derailed. The crew leapt to safety, but the locomotive plunged into the adjacent Glastonbury Canal. Removing it proved difficult because the peat bog made it impossible to position heavy lifting gear. After much thought, eventually, a month later, the water around the locomotive was diverted, and 3260 was cut into pieces weighing less than four tons, the maximum weight which could be handled by a makeshift crane, and taken away as scrap.

The S&D closed to passengers on 7 March 1966, but freight lingered on for a while afterwards on one or two parts of its routes, including the rump of the Highbridge branch. Henceforth peat was shipped by road, and the EPCL's own system was last used in 1983, and now little remains of this example of once busy

industrial narrow gauge. One of the Lister tractors – no. 42494 - is preserved at the Twyford Waterworks Museum in Hampshire.

As an ex-Fisons employee I was able to arrange for the Devon branch of the Railway Correspondence and Travel Society to visit the Eclipse Peat system, and a party of members spent an interesting and enjoyable morning viewing and travelling over various parts of it on Saturday 23 October 1965, when there was still plenty to see. The narrow gauge was still busy and extensive, and it was great fun accessing the various fields in which peat extraction was happening through gaps in hedges and crossing ditches where the track was supported by steel plates.

There were two separate parts to the system, separated by a minor road running south to north, and unconnected with each other. I asked an Eclipse Peat employee why the western section didn't have a rail connection with the eastern section, where the processing plant was also situated, which would have saved a good deal of transhipment and would have meant that peat could be transported directly into the works. The reply was that if that was to have been the case, road tax would have to be paid on all the Eclipse Peat locomotives. I have to confess that I was not convinced by this view, and I suspect that the real reason was something to do with having to agree with and pay the County Council for a level crossing arrangement, and probably any associated maintenance costs.

At the time of the RCTS visit there was still a substantial fleet of locomotives. A list of locomotives as at 23 October 1965 appears in the table below. The facts quoted are from a combination of observations on that day and notes contained in The Birmingham Locomotive Club's Industrial Locomotive Information Section (ILIS) Pocket Book B "Industrial Locomotives of Southern England", published in 1958.

All is safe and clear, and the RCTS "Special" crosses the S & D line on its way back to Ashcott. - and not an anorak in sight!
All photographs Mike Jacobs

Wheel Arrangement and Power	Manufacturer	Maker's Number	Date	Horse Power	Listed in ILIS Book	Location On 23/10/65	Notes
4w Petrol	Converted from motor cycle	None	Unknown	Unknown	Yes	Unknown	Perhaps scrapped
4w Petrol	Unknown	Unknown	Unknown	Unknown	Yes	Unknown	Perhaps scrapped
4w Petrol	Muir Hill	A125	1925	Unknown	Yes	West of highway in repair shop	Ex-unknown contractor, Avonmouth Docks
4w Petrol	Motor Rail	4604	Unknown	Unknown	Yes	East of highway in repair shop	Ex-McAlpine
4w Petrol	Lister	10498	Unknown	Unknown	Yes	Unknown	
4w Petrol	Lister	13621	Unknown	12.75	No	East of highway in repair shop	
4w Petrol	Lister	25366	Unknown	12.0	No	West of highway	Hauled RCTS train on 23/10/65
4w Petrol	Lister	34758	Unknown	8.5	Yes	West of highway	
4w Petrol	Lister	38296	Unknown	7.0	Yes	East of highway in repair shop	
4w Petrol	Lister	42494	Unknown	8.5	No	West of highway	Preserved at Twyford Waterworks Museum
4w Petrol	Lister	Unknown	Unknown	3.5	Yes	West of highway	Possibly home-made
4w Petrol	Howards & Co	Unknown	Unknown	Unknown	Yes	Unknown	
4w Diesel	Motor Rail	10633	Unknown	20.0	Yes	East of highway in repair shop	Supplied new. Possibly a replacement for a similar locomotive scrapped after an accident
4w Diesel	Ruston & Hornsby	222097	1946	20.0	Yes	West of highway in repair shop	Ex-Wm. Cory & Son Ltd, Longreach, Kent

Smokescreen at Fratton. No 76014 leaving with a Portsmouth to Cardiff working.

THE LAST STEAM-AGE FIREMAN PART 3

Roger Andrews

In 1962 Roger Andrews started at Eastleigh Shed as a cleaner.
His was to be a brief sojourn on the railway, progressing to fireman
before leaving for differing pastures.
As such he is well qualified to recall his memories as
one of the last steam age firemen.

Apart from learning when – and equally important when not - to fire. I was to discover that that long narrow fireboxes needed careful firing, whereas with the wide firebox of a West Country you just piled the coal in the back corners and under the door and they would usually steam forever. As a result I always preferred the wide firebox, that is once I had mastered the knack of getting coal into the back corners!

Soon after my trip to Salisbury I met up with another more senior fireman, who we had better call George. He was helping out on the disposal pits one afternoon and wanted to know if I would be interested in changing turns now and again. I suspect he was courting at the time and considered the hours of some of our disposal turns more suited to his intentions. George worked with a very nice chap by the name of Tom Manly, who he said would be alright about it. Naturally I agreed at once. I was to have some great times with Tom over the next nine months, most were local trip jobs, one I remember well was working trains of rubbish from Bevois Valley to a big landfill site near Woolston on the Netley line.

The next time I was on nights working on the disposal pits I got collared again. "Garth, bring your things and be quick, the running foreman wants you". I hurried to the office to be told, "There's a van train on the down main in the station, it needs a fireman off you go." I made my way to the station and there was my train, a West Country class with about nine assorted vans. I climbed aboard and met the driver. He seemed a friendly chap and obviously pleased to see me, I remember he was Ron, what happened to his fireman I do not know.

With my last trip still very fresh in my mind I asked his advice, "We go as far as Bournemouth, but don't put too much on, we only amble along and stop almost everywhere." With these wise words I had no trouble with

steam pressure, there was already a good fire so I just sprinkled a bit around the box now and again, mostly in the back corners. We reached Bournemouth in the early hours of the morning where we left the vans and then spent some time in Branksome loco' shed. When it was time to leave, it was towards Bournemouth West, then tender first back towards the main line on the other side of the triangle so that when we got back to the main line we were the right way round to head towards London.

We backed onto our train in the carriage sidings at the west end of Bournemouth station and ran them into the station. This time it was semi-fast passenger working of what was then the usual 10 coaches It stopped at all the major stations on the way to London, our job being to take it as far as Eastleigh where we would be relieved. I was nervous as well as excited, my first real passenger job.

In anticipation and under my driver's instructions, I had been steadily building up a good fire for the last half hour so that by the time we pulled into Bournemouth Central I had quite a big fire on the go. The driver seemed satisfied with this, already a very different proposition to the journey down.

We left Bournemouth just after 8 am, and despite my apprehension, the journey was quite uneventful. Station stops were Christchurch, Brockenhurst, Southampton Central and Eastleigh. I had no trouble with steam pressure and just as good, I had also now got the knack of getting coal into the back corners of the wide firebox, in fact I never had a bad trip on one of these, probably why they became my favourite class to work on, whilst they also rode very well.

We pulled into platform 2 at Southampton Central and took on water, as did all the London-bound trains. We were only booked to stop for about four minutes so we had to be quick. Water taken, a green flag from the guard and we

Previous instalments appear in SW Nos 20 and 21.

The up 'Royal Wessex' passing Eastleigh non-stop behind No 35008 'Orient Line'. A feature recalled about this and other principal early morning Waterloo services was the delicious aroma of 'eggs and bacon' that would mingle with the smell of smoke as it passed.

were away. I noticed that as we pulled out so 'The Royal Wessex' pulled into platform one, it had been following us all the way from Bournemouth.

It was not long to Eastleigh where our relief was waiting. As we came to a stop, so the 'The Royal Wessex' roared past on the up main, it would be in Waterloo three quarters of an hour before our train. What wouldn't I have given to have been on that footplate!

As we walked back to the shed to book off, my driver seemed quite pleased with my effort, while for me it was a few hours overtime and another mainline trip under my belt.

A few weeks later George came to see me, "Would I like to change turns next week?". "What is it?" I asked. He responded, "You will like this, it's an express passenger job, go passenger to Fareham and work a Brighton to Plymouth train to Salisbury." I could hardly contain myself, "Yes please", I replied, "But is Tom alright about it?" I was assured he was, so we both wrote out our exchanging turns letter to the shed master.

The procedure when changing turns was that you both had to send a written request to the shed master to change turns. I never heard of a request being refused, but it was always best to check with the other fireman to see if his driver was happy to take you, particularly if he was a more senior man. Our request was granted and I recall the last thing George said to me was to check the duty card before next week: he then gave me the duty number and that was that.

Every duty had a number and card. These cards were kept in glass-fronted cabinets in the lobby of the main building, also where the main enginemen's mess room and the running foreman's office was. The next two floors were all offices whilst over the whole of the top of this building was a huge water tank which supplied all the water columns. The duty card measured about six inches by three and had the whole duty printed on it, mostly in abbreviated form. There were several hundred duties at Eastleigh and all were displayed in these cabinets. Consequently there were always a lot of drivers in the lobby checking duty cards and making notes of times etc.

Towards the end of the week I called into the lobby to check on the duty number George had given me. I soon found the duty card and started to check it but could not believe what I was reading. According to the card, the duty started late Sunday evening, sign on just before midnight, walk to Eastleigh station, catch the mail train to Winchester and light up the shunter, that little old B4, with the same on Monday, Tuesday etc. This could not be right, so I went to the top of the card and started again. There was no mistake. "George must have given me the wrong duty number", I thought, so I went and found the running foreman. I explained my confusion and so we both went to check. It soon became clear I had been taken for a ride, although he did point out that at the end of the card there was indeed a note…'Saturday only, sign on at about midday, walk to Eastleigh station, travel passenger to Fareham, work the Brighton to Plymouth train to Salisbury etc'. I had been well and truly taken in. No wonder George had been so keen for me to check the duty card. I should have realised something was up because he had never told me to check the duty card before - he obviously didn't fancy the lighting up job for himself. I didn't really mind too much, lighting up the B4 would be a new experience whilst I would be away from the shed all week and still with the prospect of that mainline passenger job on the Saturday.

Lighting up the B4 for part of the week was 'fireman only'. I learnt later that Tom was on diesel training during the week. Thus Sunday found me signing on just before midnight: I walked up to the station and caught the mail train up to Winchester, waving to my father who was

on nights that week at St. Cross. I was a bit apprehensive because I had never had to light up an engine before, although I had seen the steam raisers lighting up enough engines at the sheds and it looked quite straight forward. I just had to work it out for myself, at least having previously spent a couple of weeks on the B4 I was quite familiar with both it and the engine shed.

On arrival at Winchester I wandered over to the shed and sorted out what to do. Having the whole place in pitch darkness didn't help much. I found the bits I needed, split sleeper wood and oily rags, and then started by placing a layer of coal on the firebars, then the rags and wood and then another layer of coal. Now the matches on the rags and wait ten minutes to make sure the fire was well alight. I could then nip back to the porters' room on the station for a cup of tea and that was the routine for the rest of the night: go back every hour to check on the fire and maybe add a few shovels of coal and then back to the porters' room. You had to be very careful not to put too much coal on, the last thing you wanted was the engine blowing off in the middle of the night, especially as the yard was in a very built-up area.

On my first night there, because there had been no shunting over the weekend, the engine was cold and it took most of the night to make steam, but the rest of the week it

The Winchester B4 at work. For many years No 30102 alternated with No 30096. Due to the sharp curve in the yard a painted wooden sign existed on the end wall of the station building, 'The only engines permitted to pass this sign on Nos 1 & 2 roads are the B4 class and 204 hp diesel.'
                                                                                    G T Storer

No 76005 on the 4.45 pm Portsmouth to Salisbury working, seen at Dunbridge on 7 September 1957.

would start to make steam within a few hours because the fire had only been thrown out at 4pm and the water in the boiler was still very hot. The only exciting part of the night was at about 3:30 am when the fast newspaper train went through. The station bell rang as it passed Winchester Junction and I always went on to the platform to watch it go through. It was always a 'Merchant Navy' class with about six or eight vans on and was a real flyer. The memory of that 'Merchant Navy' roaring through the dimly-lit station in the middle of the night, at between eighty and ninety miles an hour is one of my most abiding memories of the steam age.

But back to the B4. Towards the end of the night I would load on enough coal to last the day, so that by the time the driver and fireman arrived everything was in apple-pie order and ready to go ... including me, back to Eastleigh to sign off, and that was how the B4 was always in steam and ready.

The rest of the week went well and I got into a routine, the main problem was boredom, that was until Thursday night - Friday morning when it all went horribly wrong. I lit up as usual but halfway through the night on one of my checks I decided to put a drop of water in the boiler but could not get either injector to work. I had not had any trouble with these on the previous four nights but tonight was not my night. Try as I might they just would not work, and all the time the water in the boiler was getting lower and lower. I knew injectors could be temperamental at times but after an hour I was starting to get very anxious, what should I do? I kept trying for another ten minutes and then decided I should go back to the station and try to phone the running foreman at Eastleigh. The porter on duty got through to the loco' for me and I explained the situation to the running

foreman. I was hoping for a quick decision by him to throw the fire out, but no such luck, as he just kept telling me to go back and try again. I could not seem to get through to him how urgent the situation was. In the end I made the decision myself. "I'm going to throw the fire out" and put the phone down, and in a state of near panic ran back across the main lines to the engine shed.

When I got there the water was just in sight in the bottom of the gauge glass. But I could not throw the fire out inside the shed so the first thing was to move the B4 outside. Very gingerly I moved it outside and started to throw the fire out. Fortunately because of the injector problem I had not put too much coal on for a while and the job was soon done. What a relief, or so I thought, but then the doubts set in: did I do the right thing? Should I have tried the injectors again? Was I too hasty? Did I panic?! To the last question - yes, I did, although the consequences of dropping a plug and damaging the fire box were unthinkable,

In fact amongst footplate crews, dropping a plug was the most heinous of all crimes. Even if I did not get the sack I would have been a laughing stock for months: whoever heard of anyone dropping a plug on a B4?

I made a point of seeing the driver before I went back to Eastleigh and explained what had happened. He said one of the injectors had been playing up for some time, this just proved the importance of checking that both worked properly. All week I had only used one so when this stopped working I was in trouble. The driver didn't seem too bothered so I left the crew to it and caught my train back to Eastleigh to sign off.

I crept in to the time office back at Eastleigh to sign off, half expecting to get hauled over the coals and given a good rollicking by somebody, but nobody said a word, the running foreman saw me but said nothing so I went home. Tomorrow was my big day, no more B4, instead it was my express passenger job!

I signed on at about midday on Saturday and still nobody said anything about the B4, I met up with Tom and as we walked up to the station I told him what had happened. He said "don't worry about it, you did the right thing," I did hear the following week, when I was back on the disposal pit, that a diesel shunter had been sent up to Winchester to do the shunting and that it had also hauled the B4 back to Eastleigh for repair. That did make me feel a little better about the whole episode – and I never did hear any more about it.

Tom and I caught our train down to Fareham and just had time to cross over to the other side of the station when our working appeared, I was most disappointed. I had expected a 'West Country' but it was only a mixed traffic 76xxx Standard. Tom told me he could get any engine on this train, so that was it. One consolation was that this one was not long out of works after a general overhaul and was still quite clean and tidy, which for that class was quite rare indeed.

We relieved the Brighton men and the fireman said the usual, "She steams well, mate" and they were gone. The next surprise was the coal, it was not proper coal, but a tender full of ovoids. These burnt very quickly and gave off a tremendous heat, but also made a lot of black smoke. The trouble was when they had been tipped into the tender a lot had broken which produced a lot of fine black dust which got everywhere. The other problem was that because of their oval shape, the vibration and constant movement of the footplate, meant that for every shovelful you took off the shovelling plate, two or three followed and we were soon knee-deep in the things. You just couldn't stop them pouring off the shovelling plate.

We were soon away from Fareham and took the left-hand branch that took us through Netley and out on the main line at St. Denys. I must say that '76' Standards did steam well on its diet of ovoids. I just kept shovelling them just inside the door and the vibration and blast sent them all over the firebox. Tom shouted over, "Don't put any more on for a while. We don't want to make too much black smoke or blow off in Southampton Central."

We pulled into platform 4 which was packed with people, most of whom seemed to be for our train. The stop was about three minutes and then we were off again, and as soon as we were away from the station I started baling in the ovoids again. Past Millbrook, then to Redbridge where we took the right hand branch towards Salisbury via Romsey. Tom really had to thrash our Standard along, they weren't really built for express passenger work, having a high running board and small wheels. They always looked quite odd at speed and anyone who has ridden on one will know how they rattled, banged and crashed along. Like all Standard types they were very hard-riding and very noisy, whilst in the middle of all this bedlam was me chasing

ovoids all over the footplate and shovelling them into the firebox, but did that Standard steam! Even with the injector on it certainly liked ovoids, that's for sure.

As we roared through Dean, Tom shouted above the din, "You've probably got enough in the box now to take us to Salisbury", and so we did. I must say I was quite relieved to sit down for a while; I was as black as a crow and had worked up quite a sweat trying to round up all those ovoids. Quite a lot had also already gone over the side. We joined the main line at Tunnel Junction, then down through Fisherton Tunnel and finally ran into platform 3 at Salisbury. I jumped down and uncoupled and we ran off to Salisbury shed passing a 'West Country' waiting to back on to our train and take it on.

I am sure that being inexperienced I had made much harder work of the run than was necessary but it had been great fun and we had not been short of steam which was the most important thing. After about an hour in Salisbury loco' shed it was time for our return working, a freight back to Eastleigh via Chandlers Ford. We left the loco' shed and ran back through the station to the goods yard and backed on to our train. Tom advised me to do as I had done on my last trip back from Salisbury, which was to make up the fire level with the bottom of the fire-door and taper it to a few inches under the brick arch and then half a dozen round the box just before we left.

The trip back to Eastleigh was a carbon copy of the last trip back from Salisbury, once on the branch we ran most of the way back to Eastleigh with very little for me to do except enjoy the scenery. I do seem to remember I put a bit on this time but that was because the ovoids burnt away a lot quicker than normal coal and we arrived back at Eastleigh at about 6 p.m.

We left our train in the yard and ran light engine back to the loco' sheds where I disposed of the engine. It really had been a great day and well worth that week of lighting up the B4. It was also the last time I worked with Tom who had been a great driver to work with. Soon after this there was a move up and I left the ashpan gang. It had certainly been a lot more interesting than I thought it would be and a very good grounding for a young fireman. Apart from engines I learnt all about how the shed operated, because you were involved with so much of the day to day running of the shed. It was also confidence-building.

I was sad to leave Jimmy, I could not have wished for a better mate in my first year but it was time to go. My mate in my new gang was a young driver, Dave Thurman. We had a huge variety of work in this gang, which had a 52-week roster. This meant we went to work at a different time every week of the year, most of which seemed to be at odd hours throughout the night.

We went to places like Bournemouth, Portsmouth and Salisbury. A lot was mundane local work, although one job that sticks in my mind was a mid-morning turn - which made a change. We walked up to Eastleigh station and relieved a Nine Elms crew on a morning Waterloo to

Steam had two more years to survive when this view was taken at Bournemouth Central on 14 June 1965. The engines are Nos 76019 and D6522.

Southampton passenger train, always with a 'West Country' and worked it down to Southampton Central. Leaving the coaches we ran light engine back to Eastleigh but before disposing of our engine we did a few hours carriage shunting.

Another turn I liked was also a day turn. We prepared a 76xxx Standard and ran light engine to Eastleigh East yard to pick up a mixed freight train to Bournemouth. Here we were relieved by a Bournemouth crew and we in turn relieved another Bournemouth crew on a 'West Country'. We sat on the through line at Bournemouth Central for a while to allow a couple of London trains to come and go, and then it was our turn. Our carriages were propelled into platform 1 by the carriage shunter and we ran through the station and backed on to our train. It only consisted of five carriages and was an all stations local to Eastleigh. Once back at Eastleigh we took the coaches into the carriage sidings and ran light back to the loco shed.

The last time I did this turn we had an original 'Battle of Britain' class, *74 Squadron*, externally very shabby but it ran like a well-oiled sewing machine. What

did amuse me though was when we got up any sort of speed the wind got behind the air-smoothed casing and caused it to ripple along the whole length of the boiler, it looked as if the side was going to come off. I went over and had a look at Dave's side but this looked even worse than mine. I can't remember where this loco' came from but it was not an Eastleigh engine. That was the only time I remember seeing it: according to its history it was scrapped later that year.

Towards the middle of 1964 I was offered another job, a job in a million, but what a dilemma it put me in. I was really enjoying my work on the footplate and I was working with a great driver. The trouble was, if I refused this new job I would never get another chance. For weeks I thought long and hard. Dad was horrified at the thought of me giving up, whilst my driver tried to persuade me to stay so did the footplate inspector, the same one who had taught us in the classroom those years before.

In the end I had to make a decision and that was to try this new job. If I hadn't, I would have had doubts for the rest of my life. I think the one deciding factor was the 52-week roster on the railway and all the night work: hence I reluctantly handed in my notice.

My very last trip on the footplate was on the Portsmouth mail. We signed on about midnight and walked up to Eastleigh station where our mail train was already in at platform 4. We relieved the crew who were already on the engine – another 76xxx Standard. We were soon under way and stopped at Botley, Fareham, Portsmouth Town and Portsmouth Harbour. After a while we shunted the stock out of the station, but I can't quite recall where we parked it. Once this was done we ran light engine back to Fratton loco' shed and left our engine on the disposal pit.

The engine for our return working had been prepared for us, it was an old N class or 'Woolly'. The return working was an early morning passenger train from Portsmouth Town to Eastleigh, I'm pretty sure it was mainly for railway workers at the carriage and loco' works. We left Fratton loco' just as dawn was breaking and went to the carriage sidings to pick up our train of eight coaches and then ran to Portsmouth Town station.

I must say it was a well patronised train, every station was packed on the way back to Eastleigh. But that poor old 'Woolly' must have been not very far from the scrapyard. My last footplate trip was also the roughest from a riding point of view I'd ever had. The axle-boxes must have been well-worn with terrible banging and hammering on the footplate. Despite this it was the cab which really made us laugh, everything was loose with the cab itself seeming to be trying to detach itself from the boiler and tear itself to pieces. The noise was also indescribable, yet that engine did steam, although I suspect it would have terrified the life out of any casual footplate observer. . . and that was that.

It had been an amazing few years that I would not have missed for anything, I just wish it could have gone on for another year or two. Looking back to the mid-1960s, the running shed was like a working museum, the shed and all the work practices had not changed much since the place was built in 1903 but what an experience. I often wonder what a health and safety man would make of a large running shed like Eastleigh with its 15 roads, each with a pit and the constant movement of engines in the smoke-filled interior which was very poorly lit. There wasn't a high-visibility vest or jacket anywhere in sight. Then what about the disposal pits where seventeen-year-old lads moved all the engines down there in between jumping down to rake out the ashpans . . . the mind boggles.

Soon after I left the railways I learnt to drive and passed my test. I was able to buy a car outright with the money I had saved whilst working as a fireman - if you worked a week of nights and a weekend you could earn almost twenty pounds a week - which was a small fortune for a nineteen- year-old back in 1964. The only trouble was, you never got around to spending any of it, as we always seemed to be either working or in bed, oh the joys of shift work!

If I wasn't busy I would sometimes take my Dad to work: he was still a signalman at St. Cross and would remain there until the box closed in 1969. I would stop for an hour to watch the trains just as I had done those few years ago. The 'West Countries' and 'Merchant Navies' were still thundering past the box on their way to London Waterloo and although I was happy in my new job, how I envied those firemen, because I never did fulfil my ambition, which was to go all the way to London as a fireman.

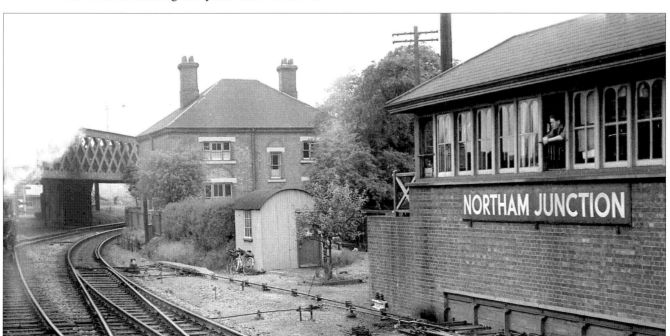

A sight familiar to generations of locomen and passengers alike. Northam Junction and the commencement of the sharp curve to Southampton Central. The signalman here needed to be a hardy soul, certain roads in the immediate area during steam days being slightly less than salubrious. .

Above - As noted in SW21, No. 70009 *"Alfred the Great"* was briefly allocated to Nine Elms for working the Bournemouth Belle – although other services were diagrammed. On 24 May 1951, the then brand new locomotive powered a special trip to Eastleigh Works and Southampton Docks for the Institute of Mechanical Engineers. This was the first recorded trip of a Britannia on the Southern Region. *Below -* Here the 8.54am Waterloo-Eastleigh is seen passing Vauxhall in pouring rain with a train of six coaches (three Maunsells and three Bulleids) in tow. Hardly an onerous first duty! Of note is the skyline – now dominated by the MI6 building and modern office blocks. (See timings on p75).

D. Cullum C993 / The Lens of Sutton Association.

More 'BRITS' - and other BR Standards
Mike King

Opposite bottom - *The weather had changed completely by the evening as No. 70009 enters Waterloo with the return 5.23pm from Southampton Old Docks – just after 7pm. The locomen of blue-liveried MN 35007 on the left are clearly interested, as is the young fireman visible on the right, who has just photographed the locomotive himself. Does anyone know his identity? Or, if you are reading this yourself please let the editor know. Note that just one extra lamp bracket has been welded to the right-hand deflector stay (there is no corresponding bracket on the left) to carry the usual Bournemouth or Southampton Terminus headcode disc (seen in use in the earlier picture). How long did the loco retain it?*

D. Cullum C994 / The Lens of Sutton Association.

Above - *Seen on Bournemouth shed on 7 June 1951, No. 70009 keeps company with one of the local B4 dock tanks (either No. 30086 or 30096) used on shed pilot duties or the Poole and Hamworthy quay branches. Presumably the Britannia has worked down on the Bournemouth Belle (12.30 ex-Waterloo) and would be laying over before the return run at 4.35pm from Bournemouth West. There was only a short layover between the duties and for this reason on some occasions the loco would be serviced at Branksome S & DJR shed and turned on the triangle leading to Bournemouth West. The fact that the loco is still facing "down" means that it has either only just arrived and has yet to use the shed turntable or that it will return light to Bournemouth West via Branksome station, enabling it to face London for the return journey. No additional lamp brackets are attached to the tender rear.*

SLS188

Opposite top - *No. 70014 "Iron Duke" this time – the other example of the class allocated to Stewarts Lane from 1951 until 1958 – again seen when new on 4 August 1951 crossing the Medway bridge and entering Maidstone East with a boat train for Dover and showing one of the newly fitted disc brackets in use. This was the third preferred boat train route between Victoria and Dover – the more usual ones being via Chatham or via Tonbridge, although there were several more permutations for getting through the SE London suburban area. The train will comprise the usual motley and ill-assorted collection of stock typical of SE Division boat trains of the period, with the leading coach a SECR "Continental" brake third followed by a Bulleid open third and Maunsell vehicles. Occasional LSWR "Ironclads" could still be seen, plus Pullmans with a utility van or two at the rear. Given another year or so, BR standard Mk1 vehicles would be added to the formations to give even more variety. At this time Maidstone was the limit of the outer suburban electrification – by either route to Maidstone East or West stations.* D. Cullum C1066 / The Lens of Sutton Association.

Opposite bottom - *"Iron Duke" again, this time on a down Ostend boat train at Petts Wood Junction, having left the ex-LCDR main line and joining the ex-SER line for the run down through Tonbridge and Ashford, on 28 March 1953. Again to harp on about headcode brackets, note that the crew have used the two deflector stay positions for the discs instead of the correct positions over the buffers although extended brackets in these two positions are visible so maybe there was an issue with lost discs? Whatever the reason, the signalmen have not been confused and have set the correct road at Bickley Junction. The stock is too far away for much positive identification, but the leading coach is a Bulleid semi-open brake third with mostly Maunsell restriction 1 and 4 vehicles behind – quite a tidy formation. Only two are definitely in crimson lake and cream.* D. Cullum C1638 / The Lens of Sutton Association.

Above - *And now for something slightly different! The 9F 2-10-0s were introduced in 1954 and later became regular, if not exactly common performers on the Southern Region. By 1957 thought was being given to using them on inter-regional freights into Feltham yard and a trial trip was arranged. Here we see 15A's (Wellingborough) 92127 on the turntable at Feltham on 24 April 1957, being observed by various officials from, no doubt, the CME and P. Way departments. There was clearly not a lot of room to spare and there was some overhang at each end - Feltham's table was 64ft 9in long and this was exceeded by the 9F's 66ft 2in over buffers so some care would be needed. Nicely clean for a 9F – they were more commonly absolutely filthy but the loco was quite new at the time of the test run and had probably been sent over from Cricklewood where it would have arrived with a coal train from the Midland main line.* D. Cullum C2983 / The Lens of Sutton Association

More 'BRITS' - and other BR Standards

Opposite top - Having been turned, the loco is now standing on the "coal road". Presumably no problems were experienced as other locomotives of the class subsequently worked into Feltham. Five were allocated to Eastleigh for working the Fawley-Bromford Bridge oil trains between 1961 and June 1963, as seen in Roger Andrews' article in SW21, but following dieselisaton of the turns all five (Nos 92205/6/11/31/39) were briefly reallocated to Feltham before being sent away to York three months later. Several others, including "Evening Star" worked over the Somerset and Dorset line during 1962 and 1963 and might have ventured onto Southern lines. Others could be seen on freights and inter-regional summer services, mostly from the Western Region while during 1965/66 a few from other regions were repaired at Eastleigh Works. One of these (no. 92242) turned up at Waterloo on a Saturdays only passenger service from Bournemouth Central at least twice during August 1966.   *D. Cullum C2984 / The Lens of Sutton Association.*

Opposite bottom - One of the Eastleigh-allocated engines; No. 92205 is seen awaiting the road at Chard Junction with an up train of 4-wheeled stone hoppers from Meldon Quarry on 2 February 1962, having presumably taken over from a Mogul or S15 at Exeter Central. Sight of one of these engines on the West of England main line was most unusual but shows that other duties other than the Fawley oil trains were worked. The final working over the route was that of "Evening Star" on 20 September 1964, hauling a Southern Counties Touring Society "Farewell to Steam" enthusiasts' special from Waterloo to Yeovil, Axminster and Seaton Junction. During this tour the loco was serviced at Yeovil Town shed – quite likely the only time the class was seen there.   *A.E. West R3764.*

The timings for the run of Thursday 24 May were (Passing times shown in italics):

Waterloo	8.54 am dep	
Worting Junc	*9.58*	
Winchester Junc	*10.14*	
Eastleigh	10.25	arr
	11.55	dep
Northam Junc	*12.01*	
So'ton Dock Gates	*12.06*	
So'ton Old Docks	12.15 pm arr	

The engine remained with the train at Southampton returning to the following times:

So'ton Old Docks	5.23 pm dep
So'ton Dock Gates	*5.28*
Northam Junc	*5.33*
Eastleigh	*5.43*
Winchester Junc	*5.55*
Worting Junc	*6.13*
Waterloo	7.12 pm arr

Right - *From the footplate of a Standard (this one is Class 4 4-6-0 No 75075, on the 7.18 am Waterloo to Salisbury semi-fast, approaching Hampton Court Junction, 19 April 1967. This train was one of the few main-line steam hauled services to call at Surbiton (due 7.36), so the picture would have been taken after 7.40 am.*

G S Cocks

THE EAST KENT RAILWAY IN ITS DYING YEARS

Terry Cole

The East Kent was conceived before World War I to link a number of collieries in the East Kent coalfield to Richborough Port. Unfortunately most of the schemes were too optimistic and the mines never reached production. Only Tilmanstone colliery at the southern end of the system was a viable undertaking.

The first section of line left the former SECR Canterbury – Dover route at Shepherdswell and proceeded north through Golgotha Tunnel and cutting, by far the biggest engineering works on the line, to a junction at Eythorne with a branch to Tilmanstone. This was open by the end of 1911. By the autumn of the following year the line had reached Eastry and by the end of the year had branched west to reach Wingham colliery. Instead of heading directly for Richborough the plan was to extend the line to Canterbury. However, like many ambitious railway schemes this was never achieved, and instead the line terminating 'in a field' at Wingham, Canterbury Road. Meanwhile as part of the war effort, a massive military port was being constructed to the north at Richborough and the EKR already had authority to construct a line to there. This opened to goods traffic at the end of 1916 but unfortunately

it had largely 'missed the boat', for after the war Richborough ceased to be a 'great port' and traffic declined sharply. Furthermore the new owners wanted nothing to do with a ramshackle outfit like the East Kent Railway. To compound matters permission to run passenger trains to Richborough had been refused due to the unsatisfactory nature of the bridges over the River Stour and the Southern Railway Ramsgate to Dover route. In an effort to offset dwindling receipts, passenger trains were run on the Richborough branch from the end of 1925 but only as far as Sandwich Road. This venture was a failure and the service was withdrawn in the autumn of 1928. For the rest of its existence the EKR struggled along with meagre agricultural traffic, a tiny passenger revenue and its mainstay: the coal traffic over the short distance from Tilmanstone to Shepherdswell. The line was nationalised in 1948, much to the relief of its shareholders who got compensation, and the remaining passenger services were withdrawn on 1 November of that year.

These photographs were taken on Bank Holiday Monday 4 August 1947 near the end of the line's independent existence.

Left - The eastern end of Golgotha cutting taken from above the tunnel mouth. What the wagons in the picture are doing is not clear.

Right - A close up of the starting signal at Shepherdswell, looking north.

Above - A general view of the station at Eythorne looking north.

Opposite bottom - Shepherdswell EKR station was situated in a cutting on a spur separate from the mainline station which lay away to the left. In this view looking north the carriage and loco sidings can be seen in the middle distance. The two sidings are full of goods and passenger stock (the run-round loop was beyond the signal) and an ex-LSWR corridor coach is on passenger train duty at the end of the platform. By a process of elimination from other photos in Rolling Stock File No 23, (p83 et.seq), I think this is no.6 ex-SR 3128 which came to the EKR in February 1946 and was withdrawn in 1948.

Top - *A close up of the station building at Eythorne with the branch to Tilmanstone Colliery diverging to the right.*

Middle - *The station building at Eastry, where the Wingham and Richborough lines diverged was rather more substantial as was the platform.*

Bottom - *The ground frame hut cum signal box at Eastry. This is of a more recent construction replacing an earlier timber one on the same site.*

Opposite top - *This is Poison Cross Halt which saw less than three years service. If this was a block post as I believe it was, the next section would be Poison – Sandwich! The wagon provides evidence that there was at least some traffic at this date.*

Opposite middle - *This photo of the next halt, Roman Road, makes Poison Cross look in positively pristine condition*

Opposite bottom - *Beyond the next halt, Sandwich Road, the line continued to Richborough Port with a halt constructed by the A256 road near Richborough Castle. This was never opened. The advertisement boards which still stand facing the road were the only source of revenue ever received from this station.*

On 4 January 1951 members of the Central Transport Consultative Committee inspected the line to review its proposed closure.

The members of the Inspection Party were;

Representing the Central Transport Consultative Committee
Major Egbert Cadbury   - Chairman
Miles Beevor, Esq   - Member
G. Cole Deacon, Esq   - Secretary

Kent Farmers' Union (Ash & District Branch):
R.G. Linnington, Esq   - Chairman*
V.R.R. Stythe, Esq   - Secretary*

The Railway Executive Southern Region
F.J. Wymer, Esq   - Assistant Chief Regional Officer
N.L. Collins, Esq   - Act. Dist. Traffic Supt. (Orpington)
F.I.S. Gill, Esq   - Dist. Engineer (Ashford)*

* Joining the party at Dover Marine Station.

The party left Victoria in reserved accommodation on the 9.30am Boat Train (light refreshments available) arriving at Dover Marine at 11.15am.

Here they boarded a special train formed of saloon No 1S departing at 11.27am with arrival at Shepherdswell at 11.45am. The train left Shepherdswell to travel over the EKR at 11.55am calling at each intermediate station for two minutes and arriving at Wingham Canterbury Road at 12.58pm. (They did not travel up the Port Richborough branch). From here they were whisked away by car at 1.0pm to the Bell Hotel at Sandwich for lunch. After this they were conveyed by reserved accommodation in an ordinary train leaving Sandwich at 3.58pm and travelling via Dover Priory and Folkestone Central (tea available after Folkestone Central) arriving back in the Capital at Waterloo East (6.16pm) or Charing Cross (6.20pm).

This information is taken first hand from a copy of the official programme for the event in my possession and provides an intriguing glimpse into the inner workings and decision making in the early BR period.

Whatever the discussions were over that lengthy lunch, all traffic north of Eythorne ceased on 1 March 1951, traffic to Wingham Canterbury Road having already ceased on 25 July the previous year, (the line still presumably being maintained). The Port Richborough branch had been completely abandoned on 1 Jan 1950. Coal continued to be transported from Tilmanstone to the junction with the SECR at Shepherdswell until April 1984.

A partly completed loop near Richborough Castle. The line was still nominally open, the Richborough branch not closing until 27 October 1949, but it is doubtful if any traffic was using this end of the branch by the time these photos were taken. [All Terry Cole Collection]

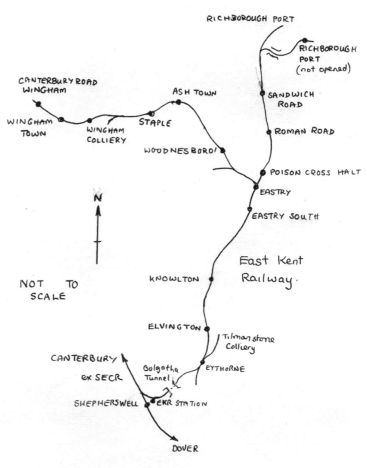

Top left - *East Kent Railway Trespass Notice at Eythorne.*

Bottom left - *Double arm starting signal at the junction at Eastry. the top arm applies to the left hand route to Wingham and the lower arm to the line to Richborough.*

Terry Cole's Rolling Stock File No. 23

The East Kent Railway

The East Kent Railway, like all of Col. Stephens' lines, acquired a motley collection of rolling stock over the years. Identifying individual items on a particular line often presents a problem due to stock being moved between the different concerns and the railways' records often being rather vague. In the case of the East Kent Railway published information is at times contradictory with coaches appearing in some sources and not in others. This is not helped by at least one case of two coaches having the same number at the same time! The EKR also numbered its coaches by means of screw on numerals which if removed left little more than a shadow.

This set of photographs was taken on Bank Holiday Monday 4 August 1947 and covers almost the entire passenger stock fleet. With the published information and by a process of elimination it has been possible to put together what is, I hope, a definitive portrait of the EKR's stock as it was in its final years.

* All the withdrawal dates quoted are rather hypothetical and differ according to which source of information you believe. Clearly much of the stock had been out of service for some time, I guess from before WWII in some cases. It was however clearly still surviving, albeit totally unserviceable, in summer 1947. More information would be most welcome.

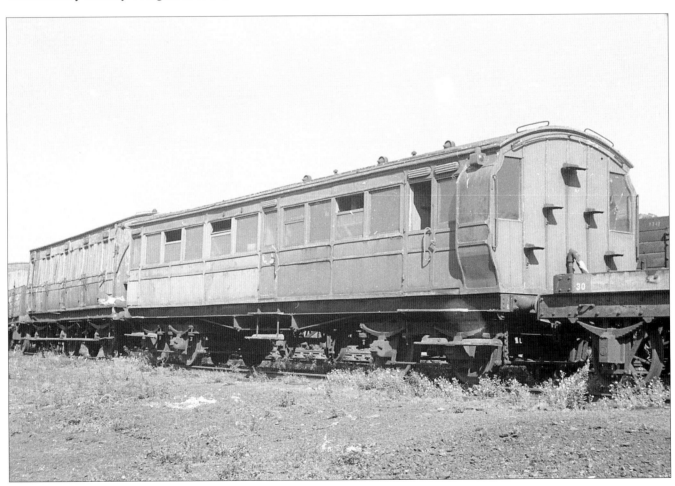

This is Bogie Open Brake Corridor Composite No 1 built by Pickering in 1905. Ex-KESR No, 17, it was transferred to the EKR around 1912 for the commencement of passenger services and withdrawn in 1948*. It was originally painted light brown.

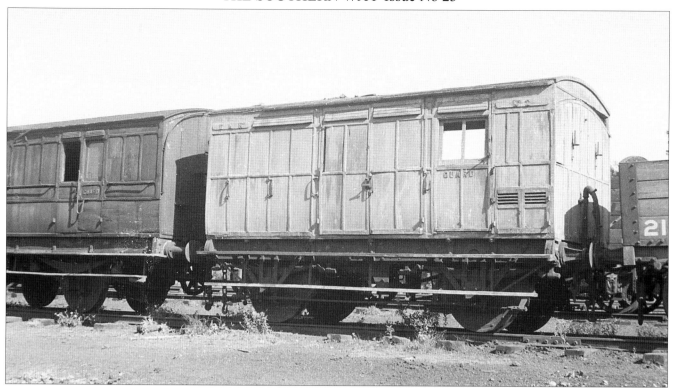

No. 2, a 4-wheel Full Brake originally built for the North London Railway. As KESR no 14 it was transferred to the EKR around 1912 and withdrawn in 1946*.

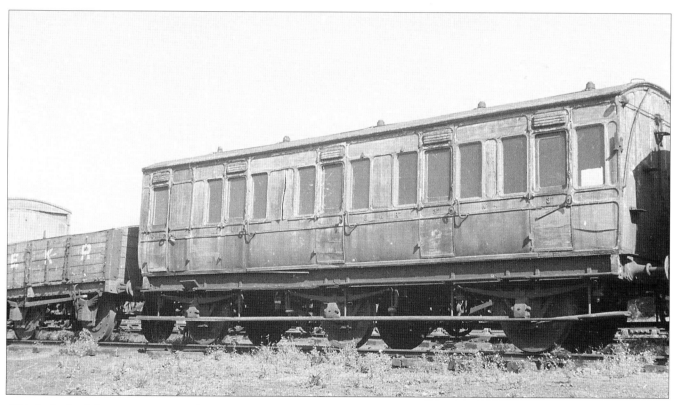

This is 6-wheel 4-compartment Brake Composite No. 4, built in 1885 for the Midland Railway. It arrived on the EKR about 1919 and was withdrawn in 1948*. The two nearest compartments show evidence of what may have been the original 3rd class painting. The EKR class numbering (3) can be seen in the screw-on numbers in the panels immediately below the droplights.

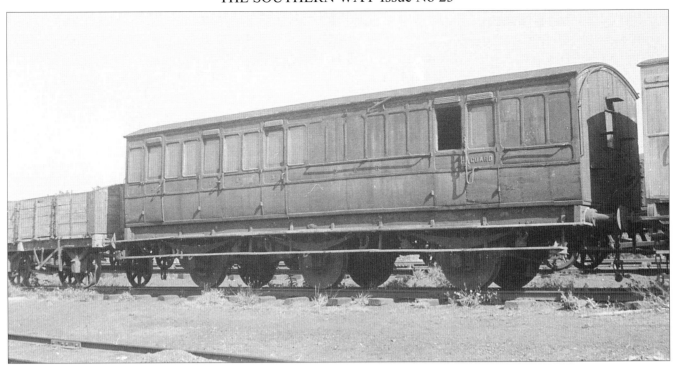

I think this is the first coach No. 5 which was a 6-wheeled 3-compartment Brake Composite built c1885 for the LSWR. It came to the EKR in 1919 and was withdrawn in 1948.The screwed on number has been removed which would be consistent with another vehicle taking its identity.*

This is the second No. 5, a 5-compartment Brake Corridor bogie coach built in July 1911 for the LSWR, later becoming SR No. 3126. It was purchased by the EKR in February 1946 together with sister coach No. 6, ex-SR No. 3128, which was on passenger train duty on the day the photos were taken. Judging by the state of the other coaches this 'upgrade' came none too soon! Both were repainted dark green on arrival and were withdrawn on the cessation of passenger services at the end of October 1948.

This sad coach is No.7, a 4-wheeled 4-compartment Third (ex First), built in 1879 for the LCDR, becoming SECR No. 2410. It arrived on the EKR in 1921.** I think the coach on the left is No.8, a 4-wheel 4-compartment Third built 1886 for the LCDR, becoming SECR No. 2737. It too came in 1921.** Both coaches were withdrawn in 1947.** On the right is coach No. 9 which we will see in a moment.

Coach No. 9, a 4-wheel 3-compartment Brake Third built 1880 for the LCDR, becoming SECR No. 3268. It came to the EKR in 1940(?) and was withdrawn in 1947.**
** Another source says these 3 coaches were purchased in 1923 and out of use by 1937. [It also says they were scrapped by 1945!]. These dates seem more plausible given their condition.

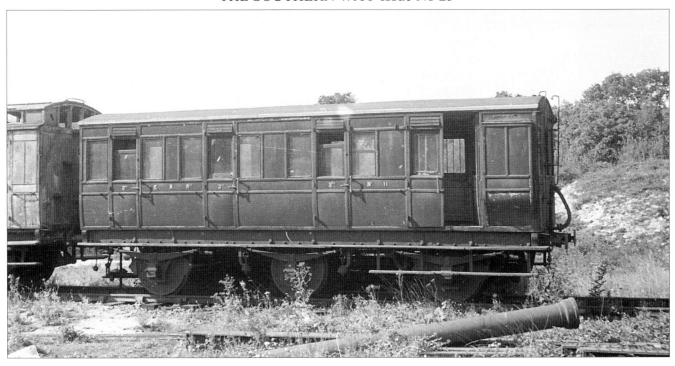

No. 11, a 6-wheel 3-compartment Brake Composite built 1891 for the LCDR, becoming SECR No. 2691. It came to the EKR c1927 and was withdrawn in 1948. Certainly it shows evidence of recent repainting, probably in the dark green any serviceable stock was given at the time. Coach No. 10 was similar. One source gives a coach No. 12, a 6-wheel 3rd of the same vintage.

I regret I don't have a photo of coach No 3, variously described as a 4-wheel ex- LCDR 1st or a 4-wheeled ex-Cheshire Lines Committee Composite! However since its body was recorded as being used as a bungalow after withdrawal in 1946 it may already have gone.

Bottom - *One photo of the antique collection of goods stock: 4 plank open wagon No. 29 complete with primitive wooden brake blocks. Unfortunately our photographer did not take any more.*

[All photos Terry Cole Collection]

In 'Southern Way No 22' (April 2013) we ran an article on 'The Eastleigh Graveyard'. Hardly was the ink dry when we received a most interesting follow-up from John Burgess.

"The Eastleigh Graveyard article reminded me of an article in an old Meccano Magazine and after trawling through a stack of yellowing and well thumbed copies I found it (October 1951). I attach a scan showing the dismantling of L11 class 4-4-0 No. 30134. It is clearly written by somebody who worked at Eastleigh (could "Shed Superintendent" perhaps be S.C. Townroe?) and gives some contemporary insight into the way in which this work was managed and carried out. Did they really sell locomotive nameplates for no more than scrap value?"

THE MECCANO MAGAZINE: *The Scrapping of Locomotives,* by "Shed Superintendent".

"It is always a sad sight to see old, rusty locomotives forlornly waiting to be scrapped, or as the Americans say queued up for the "blow-torch," the oxy-acetylene cutting apparatus used during scrapping operations. By way of consolation it is amusing to speculate upon the future of the metal which will be sold and melted down for use again. Some of the steel may find its way into new locomotives, so that new engines will arise from the ashes of the old ones. It is more likely that it will be used for making something entirely different; even for Meccano parts. Who knows?

Engines are earmarked for scrap a long time before they reach the final stages. Decision may be made to abolish a whole class or type of engine, on various grounds - age, unsuitability for modern traffic, numerical inferiority or non-standard design. Usually, when new locomotives are built, a similar number of old ones is marked down for disposal. If the old ones are of a type that can be sold intact, such as small shunting engines useful in private sidings, they are put up for sale "as found," in the condition they happen to be in at the time of sale. Otherwise, engines listed for scrapping are allowed to run until they are worn out; but even then each engine may not be entirely cut up. Certain parts, such as crank axles, for example, will be preserved if in good condition, and another engine of the same type, which may suffer a broken axle but is not worn out in other respects, will have the good axle transferred to it. This cannibalisation process is carried on until there is no further object in retaining any spare parts.

The initial stage in the scrapping procedure is the removal of all special fittings, such as mechanical lubricators and vacuum ejectors, and material that can be used on other engines of any type, such as copper piping, and buffers. All brass work is then stripped off, either for melting down or, in the case of engine nameplates, perhaps for sale as souvenirs to railway enthusiasts who are prepared to pay the full market value of the metal. The remainder of the engine except the boiler, consists mainly of steel or cast iron, and these metals must be separated as far as possible by selective cutting operations with the oxy-acetylene torch. The boiler will be removed and, as it contains valuable copper, cut up independently. The engine frames, cab, tender and so on, will finally be cut into pieces small enough to be loaded by a crane into an ordinary open railway wagon, for despatch to the scrap merchant or steel foundry.

Lest it be thought that scrapping is a job for any "engine butcher" it should be pointed out that skill and experience are essential, and the men responsible for this work have been fully trained in locomotive manufacture and repair. They are able to identify the various metals correctly, for obviously the steel merchant does not pay for lumps of cast iron! They know just where to make the cuts without waste of material, or of oxygen and acetylene gas, and without danger to themselves from sudden collapse of the severed portions. It is fascinating to watch an expert with the blow-torch, for he is able when necessary to burn out the rivets joining two parts together without damaging in any way the metal through which the rivets pass, in order to reclaim any particular part in good condition for further use.

The men engaged on this work can only be released from the repair shops at intervals and it is therefore customary to allow a number of old engines to accumulate in some little used siding until an attack can be made on them. These sidings are a mecca for the enthusiast, who takes his last chance of some old favorites."

Editor's note - "Shed Superintendent" was indeed 'SCT'. For several years he penned a number of articles in the 'MM' under a number of pseudonyms.

Scrapping begins with the removal of the chimney and smokebox of L11 4-4-0 No 30134.

A 'J' Class Postscript by Sid Sponheimer

"I was interested in your item on the above in issue 20, as I knew I had a couple of pictures of my grandfather taken with one such engine - attached. He was an engine driver at Bricklayers Arms so I imagine it was taken there. An interesting point is

that it shows SOUTHERN but still with the SE&CR number (as does the engine on p86 of SW20 and was eventually the last one in service.

My grandfather had a mention on page 104 of the Bradford Barton book " Engineman SR" by M Jackman due to our unusual surname and unbelievably, many years later in the 1960s, I was standing waiting to ask permission to go round the shed at Hither Green, when the driver in front of me at the shedmasters office gave my surname when asked his name. I asked him if it really was his name and was told " No - we always say that as a wind-up"!

EXTRACTS FROM THE SOUTHERN RAILWAY TRAFFIC CONFERENCE MINUTES

Compiled by David Monk-Steel

SOUTHERN RAILWAY TRAFFIC OFFICERS CONFERENCE No 183

Minutes of a meeting held at Waterloo Station on Monday 21 July 1930

Present – Sir Herbert Walker, Messrs G S Szlumper, E C Cox, A D Jones, F Bushrod, J B Elliot, E J Missenden, H E O Wheeler, W J England, G H Wheeler, R Buxton, F A Brant, R M T Richards, D S McBright, A White, W A Brown, C J C Latham, R L Whitworth, E Hight, L W Judd, W T Hopgood.

7119 Fatal Accidents to Servants:
Four railway servants had been killed on duty during June. Three were struck by trains and one was electrocuted on the live rail.

7120 Train Accidents:
(a) CANTERBURY WEST, WHIT-MONDAY, 9 JUNE, 1930. At 10.18 pm, when the 9.25 pm excursion train from Margate to Grove Park was being set back on the up platform line at Canterbury West, the Signalman erroneously operated No 18 up through to up platform line points, with the result that the rear coach, which was then leading became derailed, blocking the up platform line at the Sturry end of the station. No complaint of injury was made by any of the passengers. The derailed coach was detached and the train proceeded after a delay of twenty-five minutes. A rerailment was effected at 1.0 a.m. and during the interval trains booked to stop at Canterbury West were run through the station on the up through line and shunted back to the up platform line.

After arrival of the train, which was too long for the platform, at Canterbury West, it was drawn forward under the authority of No 29 shunt signal to enable passengers to alight, it having been arranged between the platform staff and the Signalman that up trains which were too long should be so dealt with and afterwards set back to clear the track. Station Foreman Roffey gave the proper bell code from the platform to the Signal Box for the shunting signal to be lowered, but failed to give the authorised code for the shunting back movement.

At the time the 9.25 pm train from Margate was standing at the up platform the empties to form the 10.10 pm train to the Elham Valley Line were on the down main line, and it was necessary to shunt them to the up through line for the passing of the 7.30 pm train from Victoria. This shunt movement made it necessary to reverse No 18 points, which was done by Signalman Woodland just as the passenger train was setting back.

Foreman Roffey is chiefly to blame for giving authority for the train to be set back before the shunt signal had been operated, whilst Signalman Woodland is to blame for moving No 18 points without satisfying himself that it was safe to do so. Both men have been cautioned, Guard T C Davis, who was in charge of the train, was content to allow the shunting movement to be made by the platform staff, and a caution has also been administered in his case.

(b) Gillingham (Dorset) 10 June – three wagons being shunted into the down sidings became derailed.
(c) Bridestowe 17 June – a ballast train became derailed whilst discharging ballast.
(d) Northfleet 27 June – A ballast train collided with a goods train being shunted from one line to another during single line working.
(e) Lyme Regis 29 June – Engine No 359 became derailed in the station due to a track defect.
(f) Walworth Dust Sidings, between Elephant & Castle and Loughborough Stations 30 June – a wagon was derailed due to buffer locking.
(g) Ashford (Kent) 1 July – a collision between light engine No A11 and an empty coaching stock train due to misreading of signals by an inspector.
(h) West London Junction 7 July – derailment of an empty coaching stock train due to mismanagement of points by the signalman.
(i) WATERLOO, 10 JULY. At 10.6 am when the 9.12 am. passenger train from Chertsey to Waterloo was entering Waterloo Station, the engine (0-4-4 Tank No. E356) and the leading coach became derailed. The passengers were detrained on to the permanent way and walked to the station. There were no cases of injury or shock. Considerable damage was done to the track and the brake work of the engine but the coach was only slightly damaged. The coach was re-railed at 12.10 and the engine at 12.50, the line at the spot being cleared at 4.30 p.m.

Groombridge station, an undated view but at a guess circa 1925. The view is looking towards the Up Main Starting signal and Junction Up Distant Signals. Notice the ghosting by the board crossing where a man has clearly moved during the exposure.
E Wallis

The road was correctly set for the train, which was travelling at normal speed to enter No.15 platform, but when between the "A" signal box and the end of the platform Driver Flint felt the engine lift and rock, and he at once made a full application of the brake. The engine came to rest with the left hand loading wheel on the ramp of No 15/16 platform, all wheels being derailed to the north of the intended road, and all wheels of the coach, with the exception of the trailing pair of the rear bogie were also derailed outside No 15 road.

On examination of the track revealed that one pair of wheels, presumably the leading driving, were derailed just after passing No 44 points, which are the last pair of facing points before entering No 15 road from the up main local line. Marks on the track indicated that the left leading driving wheel crossed over the rail just beyond No 44 points and travelled along a check rail, when the distortion of the engine caused the left trailing driving wheel to take the wrong side of an angle point, and also become derailed. The engine in its derailed state pulled the leading coach off the road and the engine became uncoupled as it came to rest. The vacuum brake pipes were still connected between the engine and the train.

The road at the spot is on a right hand curve of approximately five chains radius but owing to the lay-out, no super elevation is given. On account of the curve the road at this point is spiked 'wide of gauge' The left hand switch of No 44 points is worn somewhat on the side but is still in good condition and fit for service The top of the switch, although chipped slightly in two or three places, makes a good fit with the stock rail.

A Joint Enquiry was held, and the Officers report as follows, "Engine No E356 came out of the shops after general repairs, which included turning up of the wheels and flanges, on the 7 March 1930, and since that date has run approximately 13,000 miles. The flange of the left leading driving wheel is worn beyond the permissible limit, and has a very sharp profile.

After hearing the evidence of the staff concerned, inspecting the track work and engine wheels, and conducting certain tests with the engine, we have come to the conclusion that the derailment is attributable to the worn flange of the left hand leading wheel. This had a distinct climbing tendency, and the sharp curve at the switches, which were side worn to some extent, accentuated this and enabled the wheel to mount the rail". Fitter T F Braithwaite was aware of the condition of the flange and was responsible for allowing the engine to work the train in question, it being his intention to withdraw the engine from service on its return. He has been reprimanded for his error of judgment.

7121 Irregularities in Working:
(a) Wimbledon 6 June – the 2.45 pm Waterloo to Guildford passed Wimbledon B down through starting signal at danger without authority.
(b) Pluckley 10 June - the 9.35 pm Folkestone Harbour to Victoria passed the up advanced starting signal at danger without authority.
(c) St. Johns 18 June – 4.7 pm Dartford to Charing Cross passed up North Kent outer home signal (57) at danger without authority,
(d) Between London Bridge and Bricklayers Arms Junction 20 June – Signal A18 operated irregularly by signal lineman during a failure situation.
(e) North Kent East Junction 20 June – driver of a light engine passed No 57 shunt signal at danger without authority.

7122 Obstruction of the Line:
(a) Between Hampton Court Junction and Claygate 9 June – 1.8 pm Waterloo to Guildford struck two sheep on the line.
(b) Okeltor Crossing between Calstock and Gunnislake 9 June – 10.5 pm Bere Alston to Calstock train struck a cow.
(c) Between Aylesford and Maidstone Barracks 20 June – 6.37 pm Strood to Maidstone West struck a cow.
(d) Star Level Crossing, between Appledore and Rye 28 June – ballast train struck the gates.
(e) ERITH, 13th JULY - At 8.12 pm a saloon motor car collided with another vehicle at Avenue Road Bridge near Erith, and the car dropped on to the down line, causing a short circuit. The four occupants of the car were all injured and taken to hospital, but only one was detained. Single line working was introduced over the up line between North End signal box (between Erith and Slades Green) and Belvedere at 8.57 pm.

The motor car was hauled back to the roadway by a motor lorry, and the down line cleared at 10.20 p.m., single line working being withdrawn at 10.35 p.m. in the meantime North Kent line trains were diverted via the Bexleyheath line, leaving only the Greenwich line trains to be dealt with over the single line.

7123 Flooding of the Line:
(a) Acton Lane Junction and Bollo Lane Junction 17 June – District line services cancelled due to flooding following heavy rain.
(b) NEW CROSS, etc., 18 June. At 4.30 pm, in consequence of an exceptionally violent storm, the permanent way between New Cross and St. Johns and between Maze Hill and Westcombe Park became flooded. The colour light signalling and track circuits were affected.

The current was cut off the up and down local and down through lines between New Cross and St. Johns from 5.2 pm to 6.57 pm. Endeavors were made to restore the current to the down lines, but without satisfactory results until 9.6 pm when the down through line was charged. It was only possible, however, to pass one train at a time on that line between New Cross and St. Johns owing to the leakage current being considerably greater than the normal load. At 11.4 pm the current was restored to the down local line and at 11.35 pm all, roads were re-opened for traffic.

College Tunnel, between Greenwich and Maze Hill also became flooded and the current was cut off the down and up lines through the Tunnel from 4.50 to 5.0 pm, and from 5.8 to 5.22 pm. At Blackheath the current was taken off the down and up lines at 6.3 pm in consequence of an electric train fusing badly. The current was restored to the down line at 6.15 pm and to the up line at 7.15 pm after the electric train had been removed by an engine.

The L.C.C. Fire Brigade was requested at 7.0 pm to pump out the water from the cutting between New Cross and St. Johns, but on arrival of a Fire Brigade Officer at the scene at 8.0 pm, he declined to render any assistance on the ground that there was no actual danger to the public.

As a result of the flooding, traffic in the London East Division was entirely disorganised for several hours, the working generally being hampered by the breakdown of numerous telephone circuits.

7124 Fires on Company's Premises:
(a) AXMINSTER, 4 June 1930. At 8.29 pm, when the 7.30 pm freight train from Exeter to Nine Elms was passing through Axminster Station, the Signlman observed that the fifth vehicle from the engine, a van containing boxes of eggs and other market goods from Holsworthy, was on fire. The train was brought to a stand at the up advanced starting signal and efforts made to extinguish the fire with buckets of water, but without effect. The train was, therefore, shunted back and the vehicle placed under the water column, when the fire was subdued, the train being finally shunted to the up siding and the outbreak extinguished. The train left Axminster at 9.23 pm having been delayed fifty-three minutes. As the fire had assumed large dimensions and there was a risk of other vehicles being involved the local Fire Brigade was requested and assisted in dealing with the outbreak.

Twenty six cases of eggs were unloaded from the van and 43 cases of eggs, which had been damaged, and other salvage goods, were forwarded to London the following day. The vehicle was badly burnt and the van next attached was also damaged.

The loading of the van at Holsworthy had been completed at 3.0 pm on the day in question, and it is stated that no one entering the van at the time was smoking. The vehicle was not opened after leaving Holsworthy and the outbreak can only be attributed to a spark from the engine, probably when passing through Honiton Tunnel, the spark having apparently found its way into the interior of the van.

(b)Between Whitstable and Faversham 5 June – two wagons in 6.45 pm goods Birchington to Faversham on fire. It was thought to be caused by a spark from the engine.
(c) Bournemouth West 6 June – A fire in rubbish in the goods yard.
(d) Robertsbridge 10 June – A LMS wagon in the goods yard was on fire. It was thought to be caused by a spark from a passing engine.
(e) Between Liphook and Liss 17 June – Fire in the gangway at front of 3.50 pm Waterloo to Portsmouth. It was thought to be caused by a spark from the engine.
(f) Crowthorne 19 June – Heather packing in an empty wagon in the 6.11 pm special goods Ascot to Dover on fire. It was thought to be caused by a spark from the engine.
(g) Brighton 24 June – Lime in a wagon standing in Top Yard spontaneously combusted following leakage of a wagon sheet allowing water to contaminate the load. The top sheet was not tightly secured or supported.
(h) Bickley (Sunday) 6 July – Fire in first class compartment of empty electric train in the down sidings. Four first class compartments destroyed.
(i) Umberleigh 6 July – Permanent Way hut completely destroyed by fire.
(j) Redhill 7 July – A wagon in South Yard on fire. It was thought to be caused by a spark from a passing engine.

7125 Burglaries on Company Premises:
Four incidents, St. Helen's Quay store room, Bournemouth Central coal office, East Grinstead refreshment room, and Sutton trader's office.

7127 Compensation claims:
£23,714.0s.3d was paid in first six months of 1930, an increase of £4,256.3s.7d over same period in 1929.

Cannon Street, SECR, looking towards Borough Market Junction - undated.

7128 Demurrage Charges on Trucks and Sheets:
£5,362.4s.5d collected in first six months of 1930. £5,470.19s3d outstanding at end of May.

7129 Outstanding Goods and Parcels charges:
£607, 456.13s.3d outstanding for May 1930

7130 London Goods Cartage:
Work done for 26 weeks ended 25 June 1930
Horse Cartage (tons) Bricklayers Arms and Blackfriars 84,299, Nine Elms 74,636, Willow Walk 36,999,
Motor Cartage (tons) Bricklayers Arms and, Blackfriars 26,254, Nine Elms 79,720, Willow Walk 12,091
Average weight by horse working per day 2 tons - 11.39 cwt
Average weight by motor working per day 7 tons – 17.55 cwt

7131 London Parcels Cartage:
Work done for 26 weeks ended 25 June 1930
Horse Cartage (no. of parcels) Cannon Street and Holborn 381,112, London Bridge 767,927, Waterloo 634,007,
Motor Cartage (no. of parcels) Cannon Street and Holborn 473,341, London Bridge 131,819, Waterloo 1,256,643.

7132 Average Loading of Wagons and Trains:
Loading for 26 weeks ended 25 June 1930

	Tons Outwards	No of Wagons loaded	Average load per wagon	No of trains forwarded	No of Wagons	Average No of wagons per train
Nine Elms	362,838	109,217	3 tons 6.4 cwt	2,379	126,877	53.3
Bricklayers Arms	195,359	61,201	3 tons 3.8 cwt	3,624	133,495	36.8
Willow Walk	144.177	48,637	2 tons 19.3 cwt	905	54,714	60.4

7133 – 5 Ledger Accounts, Surplus and Losses in Booking, and Bad Debts: Discussed

7136 Engine Failures in June 1930:

No:

Western Div. 25
Eastern Div. 14
Central Div 15
Miles run per engine failure : 85,025

7137 Mileages

Submitted: -Mileage statement for the month of June 1930, compared with the corresponding period of 1929:

	Current Month	(+) Increase (-) decrease	Aggregate for Year (Six Months) 1930	(+) Increase (-) decrease
TRAIN MILES	STEAM LOCOMOTIVE ENGINES			
Coaching				
Passenger Loaded:-				
Ordinary	2,393,121	+ 79,937	14,360,878	+ 274,829
Special and Conditional	220,377	+ 27,131	509,926	- 8,617
Fruit, Milk, Fish, etc., Loaded				
Ordinary	115,083	- 911	702,130	+ 25,379
Special and Conditional	27,485	- 66	77,802	- 8,402
Empty	136,060	+ 25,898	525,061	- 24,090
Freight				
Ordinary	525,149	- 15,266	3,363,344	+ 50,569
Special and Conditional	20,669	- 5,858	130,046	- 30,377
	3,437,944	+ 110,865	19,669,187	+ 279,291
OTHER MILES				
Shunting				
Coaching -				
By Shunting Engine	139,251	+ 3,390	807,794	+ 3,221
By train	87,570	+ 4,552	470,696	+ 4,984
Freight				
By Shunting Engine	359,992	- 14,344	2,320,534	- 28,287
By train	163,648	- 4,015	1,057,426	- 8,882
Assisting Required				
Coaching	10,055	+ 4,664	46,902	+ 27,592
Freight	3,630	+ 199	23,010	+ 676
Assisting not Required	21,627	+ 3,815	100,362	+ 5,882
Light	263,731	+ 11,590	1,376,268	- 10,650
Total other Miles	1,049,504	+ 9,849	6,201,992	- 5,464
Total (excluding Departmental)	4,487,448	+ 120,714	25,871,179	+ 273,827

DEPARTMENTAL MILES

Locomotive Department	60,938	- 6,240	401,423	- 14,309
Carriage & Wagon Department	10,093	+ 136	69,021	+ 686
Stores Department	785	- 115	5,119	- 21
Ballasting (including Engineer's Service Trains)	62,306	- 15,809	410,575	- 26,154
Miscellaneous	3,408	- 598	20,884	- 417
Total Departmental Miles	137,530	- 22,626	907,022	- 40,215
Total Steam Loco Engine Miles	4,624,978	+ 98,038	26,778,201	+ 233,612
Ratio of Unproductive Miles (other and Departmental) to Total Engine Miles	25.67	-	26.55	-

ELECTRIC TRAINS

Train Miles				
Passenger Loaded				
Western (excluding Waterloo & City Railway)	436,337	+ 5,235	2,600,985	+ 41,690
Central A.C.	-	- 53,230	-	- 571,366
Eastern & Central D.C.	1,056,232	+ 83,249	6,398,544	+ 1,085,555
Waterloo & City	15,555	- 84	96,306	+ 4
Total Loaded	1,508,124	+ 35,170	9,095,835	+ 555,883
Passenger Empty				
Western	10,918	+ 1,929	58,836	+ 3,132
Central A.C.	-	- 1,326	-	- 12,850
Eastern & Central D.C.	14,698	+ 4,314	74,603	+ 23,393
Total Empty	25,610	+ 4,917	133,439	+ 13,675
Total Train Miles	1,533,734	+ 40,087	9,229,274	+ 569,558
Other Miles				
Shunting	597	- 275	3,631	- 1,877
Departmental Miles	3,937	+ 2,570	12,627	- 2,312
Total Electric Miles	1,538,268	+ 42,382	9,245,532	+ 565,369
Total Miles Steam Locomotive & Electric	6,163,246	+ 140,470	36,023,733	+ 798,981

LBSCR staff, South Croydon, c1900.

7137 Electric Car Miles:

	Current Month		(+) Increase (-) decrease	
	Loaded	Empty	Loaded	Empty
Western Section (Excluding Waterloo & City)	2,518,242	73,842	+ 159,670	+ 17,455
Central Section A.C.	-	-	- 394,065	- 9,462
Eastern & Central Sections D.C.	6,029,450	103,555	+ 684,453	+ 31,221
Waterloo & City	48,699	-	- 1,884	+ 39,214
Total				

	Aggregate for Year (Six Months) (Including Waterloo & City) 1930	(+) Increase (-) decrease
Loaded	50,608,008	+ 3,632,056
Empty	900,096	+ 102,030
Total	51,508,104	+ 3,734,086

Notes			Miles Run by Southampton Docks Engines	
	1930	1929	1930	1929
Number of Weekdays	24	25		
Number of Weekends	5	5	Coaching Shunting 1,700	1,570
Number of Sundays	1	-	Freight Shunting 20,090	21,035
Total Number of Days			Total 21,730	22,605

Miles Run by Petrol cars			Aggregate to Date	
Included with miles run by Steam Locomotives	Current Month	Corresponding Month last year	1930	1929
Passenger Loaded	1,629	-	1,629	6,892
Passenger Empty	-	-	-	15
Departmental				
Trials Trips	44	-	670	-
Engineer's	-	-	-	144
Included with miles run by Electric Trains				
Departmental	879	-	4,241	2,135
Total	2,552	NIL	6,540	9,186

The trains in the Special Bank Holiday Working Time Tables have been treated as 'Ordinary' except those booked to run if required, which have been treated as 'Special' if run.

Electric Services (D.C.) Inaugurated
Replacing Steam Services
23 September 1929 - Victoria to Sutton and Coulsdon North via Streatham Common.
The replacement of A.C. electric services by D.C. electric services is completed.

New Line Opened.
7 July 1929 - Wimbledon to Merton South
5 January 1930 - Merton South to Sutton. (Extension of Holborn Viaduct and Victoria to Wimbledon service.)

EXTRACTS FROM THE SOUTHERN RAILWAY TRAFFIC CONFERENCE MINUTES

7138 Working of Passenger Trains:
Extensive analysis of passenger train working (punctuality) for the month of June 1930 was presented. The following is a summary.
STEAM TRAINS WEEKDAYS
77,667 trains were operated, 70.51% ran right time. The average late arrival 1.31 minutes.
STEAM TRAINS SUNDAYS
7,457 trains were operated, 66.65% ran right time, The average late arrival 1.83 minutes.
ELECTRIC TRAINS WEEKDAYS
72,417 trains were operated, 78.39% ran right time, The average late arrival 0.62 minutes.
ELECTRIC TRAINS SUNDAYS
11,129 trains were operated, 82.09% ran right time, The average late arrival 0.60 minutes.

7139 Working of Freight Trains:
Extensive analysis of freight train working at principal places for the month of June 1930 was presented. The following is a summary.
DEPARTURES
Total trains run (including specials) 14,742, Average minutes late departure 1.5, Average no. of wagons per train 30.8.
ARRIVALS
Total trains run (including specials) 14,963, Average minutes late arrival 6.4, Average no. of wagons per train 29.2.

7140 Continental Traffic:
Passenger, Cargo and Motor Cars conveyed between England, France and Channel Isle etc. for month of June 1930
SR Co's steamers -   No of Passengers 162,020, Tons of Cargo 45,255, Motor Cars 1344.
Other Co's steamers -   No of Passengers 51,430, Tons of Cargo 889, Motor Cars 126.

7141 Isle of Wight Passenger and Motor Car traffic for month of June 1930:
Via Portsmouth   Passengers 271,837 Motor Cars 1,563.
Via Lymington   Passengers 29,291 Motor Cars 191.

7143 Padstow Fish Traffic:
6 months ended 30 June 1930 - 1214 tons by passenger train, none by goods train.

7144 to 7150 Salaries and Wages, Staff Changes, Hours of Duty of Certain Grades , Detection by Staff of Irregular Travelling, Staff Punishments, Staff 60 Years of Age or Over, Additional staff for Summer Traffic:
Returns were tabled and discussed.
Wages and Salaries in Locomotive Running, Traffic and Commercial departments for five weeks ended 25 June 1930 totalled £695,768.
805 additional staff would be required for Summer Traffic 1930.

7151 Forged Bank Notes:
Three forged one pound notes have been detected this year.

7152 Combined Rail and Road Bookings etc. Associated Road Companies:
The following additional interavailability of rail and road tickets have been introduced –

Devon General Omnibus and Touring Co.Ltd.	Exeter and Budleigh Salterton Exeter and Okehampton Exeter and Sidmouth Budleigh Salterton and Exeter Okehampton and Exeter Sidmouth and Exeter
Hants and Dorset Motor Services Ltd.	Broadstone and Poole Wimborne and Poole Poole and Broadstone Poole and Wimborne Lyndhurst Road and Southampton West Southampton West and Lyndhurst Road

Southdown Motor Services Ltd

The backward halves of Southdown company's tickets (Day Return and Period Return) London and Brighton are accepted at Brighton (Central) station and rail tickets issued in London on surrender of bus tickets and the payment of 2s/- adult and 1s/- Child; also the return halves of Brighton and London tickets are similarly dealt with at London Bridge and Victoria. Return halves of rail tickets are not available on the Omnibuses.

7154 Street Direction Sign

Sunbury, The Metropolitan Water Board has granted permission to attach a direction sign to the wall of their bridge spanning the Staines Aqueduct at Sunbury Cross.

7155 Post Office Telephone Facilities

Additional telephones at Maidstone and Paddock Wood in connection with Hop Pickers traffic, and at Herne Hill Goods office are authorised.

7156 BEXHILL : BEXHILL CORPORATION'S SIDING

In 1877 the London Brighton and South Coast Company laid in a siding from the down line between Bexhill Central and St Leonards West Marina Stations for a Mr. Frederick Cruttenden, he paying the cost of the work, the siding being maintained by, and at the expense of the Company.

In 1905 the Bexhill Water and Gas Company took over the siding, and in 1929 it came to notice that the Bexhill Corporation had acquired the Bexhill Water and Gas Company's property. As no agreement has previously been entered into, a document has now been prepared on the lines of the usual standard siding agreement, providing that the whole of the siding to be maintained at the expense of the Corporation, the payment of an acknowledgment rental of £1 per annum for the use of the Company's land occupied by the sidings and the application of the Bexhill Station rates for the conveyance of traffic to and from the siding.

It is recommended that the agreement be completed accordingly.

7157 CANTERBURY WEST : SIDING FACILITIES FOR CENTRAL ELECTRICITY BOARD.

REPORTED- That an application had been received from the Central Electricity Board for siding facilities to serve a Sub-Station they propose erecting on land adjoining the up line between Sturry and Canterbury West Stations.

The scheme is indicated on Plan No 41,461 and this Company will carry out the work shown in full red colour on the plan at an estimated cost of £646 which amount the Electricity Board have agreed to pay, and they undertake that the siding shall be laid in by their Contractors to the satisfaction of this Company's Engineer.

It is recommended that the matter form the subject of an agreement providing as follows.

The cost or the construction and subsequent maintenance of the siding to be borne by the Central Electricity Board. A nominal rental to be paid for the use of the Company's land occupied by the siding.

Application of the Sturry Station rates for the conveyance of traffic to and from the siding.

7158 CANTERBURY WEST: SIDING FACILITIES FOR SOUTH EASTERN TAR DISTILLERS LIMITED

Referring to Minute 6987 of the 24th March 1930, respecting siding facilities from this Company's up line between Sturry and Canterbury West for the South Eastern Tar Distillers Limited, it was reported that the Firm have requested that the siding be extended on their property, the estimated cost of the work being £59.

The South Eastern Tar Distillers Limited have offered to pay an additional £5 per annum to cover the extra expense involved, and it is recommended that the offer be accepted, the arrangement to be made the subject of a suitable supplemental agreement.

7159 CORFE CASTLE: MESSRS. PIKE BROTHERS' SIDING

Referring to Minute 6992 of the 24th March, 1930, under which the terms of the agreements dated 18th August 1902, with Messrs. Pike Brothers for their private siding at Furzebrook, near Corfe Castle, were modified to the extent of reducing the rental to 5 per cent on the original outlay in connection with the provision of the siding, providing the traffic exceeded 30,000 tons per annum, it is considered the time has now arrived that the rental payable under the agreement should be dropped.

It is recommended that a short agreement be prepared, providing for the rental being waived, the Company reserving the right to call upon Messrs Pike Brothers to pay for the maintenance of the siding for any year during which their traffic has fallen below 30,000 tons.

Opposite page - *Another of the magnificent signalling / infrastructure images from the camera of the late E Wallis. This is the Farnborough North Down Home Signal complete with repeater arm, looking north on 23 June 1928. Look out for an important announcement concerning this collection in the October issue of 'SW'.*   David Wallis

7160 EASTBOURNE. MESSRS BA1NBRIDGE AND SON'S APPLICATION RE SIDING:

Referring to the agreement dated 16th December, 1884, between the London Brighton and South Coast Company and the Eastbourne Water Company, under which siding facilities were provided from the old ba1last line, situated on the down side of the line at Eastbourne for the Water Company, the scheme for the Waterworks was subsequently abandoned and the siding came into disuse.

In 1923 the Eastbourne Water Company disposed of their property to Messrs. Bainbridge and Sons, but considerable difficulty has been experienced by the Firm in connection with the laying out of a depot. They are, however, now prepared to proceed with the re-conditioning of the siding.

Plan No.40,051 was submitted, showing the siding in brown, which requires complete renewal, but for the present Messrs Bainbridge and Son only wish the portion up to the point marked "A" on the plan to be re-laid, the cost of which, together with alterations to the fencing and gate as indicated in red on the plan, is estimated at £274. Messrs. Bainbridge and Son being prepared to do the excavating and carrying away the surplus soil.

It is recommended that an agreement be prepared, providing for cost of the renewal and alterations to fencing and gate and subsequent maintenance thereof to be borne by Messrs. Bainbridge and Son, a nominal rental to be paid for the use of the Company's land occupied by the siding and the application of the Eastbourne Station rates, plus 11d per ton with a minimum of 2s/5d per truck for the conveyance of traffic to and from the siding.

7161 MAIDSTONE. SIDING FACILITIES FOR CENTRAL ELECTRICITY BOARD:

REPORTED:- That an application had been received from the Central Electricity Board in respect of siding facilities to serve a Sub Station they propose erecting on land adjoining our down line between Maidstone East and Bearsted Stations in connection with the South East England Electricity Scheme.

Plan No.41,369 indicates how such a siding can be laid in at an estimated cost of £655 for the work shewn in full red colour, the remainder of the work being carried out by the Central Electricity Board to the satisfaction of this Company's Engineer. The Electricity Board have agreed to bear the cost of the work done by this Company, the subsequent maintenance of the siding, to pay a nominal rental for the use of the Company's land, and the application of Maidstone East Station rates for the conveyance of traffic to and from the siding.

It is recommended an agreement be entered into with the Board covering these arrangements.

7162 : New Works

The Following New Works are Recommended:-

Station	Nature of Work	No of Plan	Estimated Cost
			£ s d
Lancing Works	Provision of additional Crossover Road	40,531	445. 0. 0*
Porchester	Abolition of Crossover and Signal Box, and alterations to signals. A staff economy of £220 per annum will be effected.	69/1 394/1 456/1	1,958. 8. 0*
Ropley	Removal of loop line, abolition of Signal Box etc. and installation of Ground Frame, also provision of new crossover road. A saving of £70 per annum will result.	38,648 230/1	414. 0. 0*
Exmouth	Provision of short siding for coaling engines.	40,837	285. 0. 0*

* To be charged to Revenue - Abstract A.

Top - *No s21C167 'Tangmere' at Cannon Street, undated, but reported as 'newly built'. Corbis Images IL003035*

Bottom - *No 34094 'Mortehoe' entering Birmingham Snow Hill with a football special from Southampton in connection with the FA Cup semi-final, 27 April 1963. Ciorbis Images IL003126*

First of all, many thanks to all for their comments on recent issues, especially those who have helpfully identified the colour views of the mystery station where platform work was taking place, at the start of No 22 as being Blackwater.

Continuing on with some useful items from Richard Bell re THE BATTERSEA TANGLE. Richard starts with a pronouncement, "Dammit! I was scheming an article on this topic!" - sorry Richard you missed on this occasion, but do please have a go on something else, the subject of railways means there is plenty left - Ed.

"Lines towards Brixton etc.:- As Alan Postlethwaite says, the first line of the LCDR in the area was from Stewarts Lane Junction to Herne Hill, opened in 1862, and the high level line from Battersea Pier Junction followed in 1866, and that the LBSCR high level line from Battersea Park to Wandsworth Road was opened in 1867.

"A few weeks ago, I discovered from Adrian Grey's book on the LCDR (Middleton Press), that the part of the 1862 line from Wandsworth Road to the vicinity of Shepherds Lane became in 1867 the southern pair of tracks, used from that date by the LBSCR, and since about 1980 known as the Atlantic lines. Thus, as part of the same programme of works in 1866-67, the three new tracks of the high level route continued eastwards beside the 1862 tracks on the north side until they blended into the older tracks towards Brixton station, and the older lines were cut and joined instead to that newer part of the present Atlantic line which flies over Brixton Station.

"This explains the otherwise odd fact that at the west end of Wandsworth Road station the southern pair of tracks aligns with the routes to Stewarts Lane and Longhedge. A photograph on page 19 of "The LBSCR Elevated Electrification" (Noodle) shows this well, with the few yards of connecting track obviously out of regular use. (This may also explain why the one-time "Chatham" Up relief line began at Shepherds Lane rather than Brixton station.) (Neither J.T.Howard Turner's three volume history of the LBSCR nor the RCHS Chronology of London Railways refer to this matter.)"

Mixed Gauge to Victoria:- "The GWR required mixed gauge on the West London Extension Railway, but it was not installed on the two spurs to the LSWR, nor, almost certainly, did broad gauge trains run to the LBSC side of Clapham Junction (the platforms now used by Milton Keynes - South Croydon trains, there were no facilities there or nearby for handling broad gauge wagons).

"It was also persuaded to take a 30% share in the LCDR's Victoria Station. The necessary third rail was added to the LBSCR lines from Longhedge Junction into both Victoria stations. GWR standard gauge passenger trains began running to Victoria on 1 April 1863, and a few broad gauge trains from June, probably all to the LCDR/GWR station.

"The LCDR opened its own double line from Longhedge Junction to Stewarts Lane Junction on 7 October 1865, and its own lines from Stewarts Lane via the newly widened Grosvenor Bridge to Victoria on 20 December 1866. It was intended that these should be of mixed gauge, but (according to MacDermott's History of the Great Western Railway), the lines south of the branch to Chelsea basin were officially declared closed to broad gauge traffic from November 1866, so broad gauge trains never ran over these new LCDR lines, but standard gauge GWR trains were diverted off the LBSCR lines onto these."

Continuing from Richard, this time on the SEVENOAKS CUT-OFF, as featured in SW21. "Hither Green:-The Dartford Loop Up Through loop had certainly gone by the 1950s (when I was commuting between Orpington and Charing Cross).
R.W. Kidner (The Dartford Loop Line, Oakwood) refers to 1939, which would fit with the replacement of steam-hauled Gillingham semi-fasts from Gillingham by electrics via Woolwich: removal would have been presumably a part of the tidying-up. "

"The Sevenoaks derailment:- Jeremy Clarke has mistaken the location. The MoT Accident Report concluded that the locomotive derailed south of Dunton Green station and continued southwards at speed until it hit the eastern abutment of the Shoreham Lane overbridge and slewed into the side of the cutting beyond. Four of the coaches were

It is always pleasing to receive the odd snap-shot from the family album - as here. This was sent by John Mees but with minimal information. John comments, The photo was lent to me by my cousin. The man standing on the left is her grandfather who was killed in a shunting accident about 1927. I assume this is Eastleigh Works." (As usual any further information would be welcome - Ed.)

crushed against the centre pier of the bridge." (The Sevenoaks derailment also features in issues 7 and 13 of SW.)

Now from Alan Holmewood, "Hi Kevin, Just reading this and was interested in the Colonel Stephens free pass issued to Lt Col David Davies. I did a bit of research via Google and found the following reference: https://en.wikipedia.org/wiki/Mawddwy_Railway The relevant section is the fifth paragraph of the History section. It would seem that a Lt Col David Davies was Chairman of the Cambrian Railway at the relevant time. I believe that the Shropshire & Montgomeryshire connected with the Cambrian, so it would be reasonable for the Chairman of that Company to have a free pass.Be interesting to see what others come up with." (See SOUTHERN EPHEMERA - in SW22).

On a different track from Tony Nicholson - Trustee and Archivist, Lynton & Barnstaple Railway Trust. "I have just bought a copy of the latest issue of The Southern Way *(well it was the latest at the time - No 20 - ED)* and as a trustee of the Lynton & Barnstaple Railway Trust, my eye was immediately drawn to your Page Three feature. One of my colleagues thinks that the young lady in the archive photo might be Victoria Hopper who played the heroine in a new version of Lorna Doone filmed on Exmoor in August 1934." The L&BR Trust is a registered charity set up to rebuild as much as possible of the legendary Lynton line and is based at Woody Bay Station. Would it be possible for you to provide a copy of this striking photo for the Trust's archive - *done*.

Submitted by Stephen Phillips and taken at the recent Gala event at Woody Bay: the first time an L & B Manning Wardle in Southern livery has graced the station since September 1935.

Now from Peter Jordan, "I've just recovered a batch of photos I took in 1964 to form part of a village quiz. One of the pictures was taken inside Hollingbourne Goods Shed, of the Southern Railway crane. It's something

Hollingbourne Goods Shed.

a bit different, so please feel free to use it in Southern Way if you wish. As usual, apologies for the quality, and I regret the negative's gone missing, so a scan of the print is the best I can do!

It appears our piece on Bournemouth West (SW22) has proven rather appealing *(we do try)*, resulting first in this letter from Roger MacDonald, "Many thanks for the latest issue of Southern Way. I did especially appreciate the article on Bournemouth. I grew up in Branksome and spent many a happy on the platforms of the West Station. My mother was born opposite the Station in Queen's Road so it really was a nostalgic trip for me.

"That though is not the reason for my letter, however, and I refer to the article on Southern Ephemera in the same issue. Please refer to page 90 and the invitation to dinner with Mr Stroudley. What a coincidence this is, celebrating the completion of his 100th locomotive. And what was the locomotive? It was none other than E Class No. 110 *Burgundy*, still in existence and known as W2 *Yarmouth* on the Isle of Wight Steam Railway.

"There is, however, a little matter to resolve. The invitation reproduced in Southern Way gives the location as the Old Ship Hotel, Brighton, whereas Peter Cooper's LBSCR Stock Book [1] cites a celebratory dinner at the Royal Pavilion, Brighton, where the toast, 'the hundredth engine', was drunk in Burgundy wine by Stroudley and some of his senior Works staff.

Did Stroudley in fact have two bites of the cherry, one with foremen and friends at the Old Ship and a more formal occasion at the Royal Pavilion?"

(1)   Cooper, Peter. LBSCR Stock Book Runpast Publishing 1990 'E' Class No. 110 Burgundy pp 31-34

Now a brief note from George Hobbs (and others) re the lower illustration on p29 of SW2: re the first part of the EPB story. Here the location is not Wimbledon but more likely to have been Waterloo East.

Continuing on with Bournemouth West, from Frank Robertson (no relation that we are aware of - Ed). "I've recently received this eagerly awaited issue. The modelling of the Bournemouth West station being an on-going project of mine. It does appear, however, that the photo on page 59 of the water tower, has been reversed, and is described as being situated in the northern corner of the Goods Yard. In fact, the Tank House was situated to the south of the station throat, opposite the ramp end of Platform 1. I enclose some items that may be of interest. One of the buildings, built at the same time, and annexed to the original 1874 station, is the still partially extant 'New Station - Refreshment Rooms - Bournemouth' (West). The photos, however, were taken in 2012 by myself."

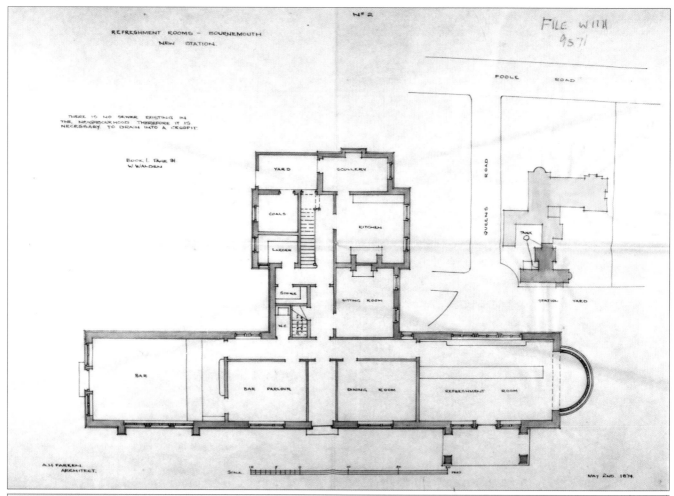

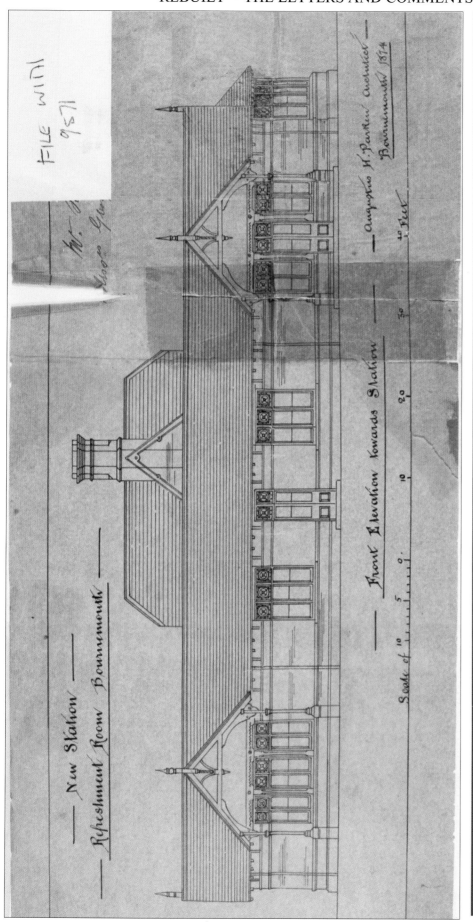

Above - With apologies for the indifferent quality, but a King Arthur on a mixed train of red and green liveried stock from 1957 was too good to miss. No 30791 recorded at Farnborough, 31 July 1957.

Above - New Milton towards Bournemouth. Another interesting combination of liveries. The carriage roof boards are just a little indistinct although the board on the cantrail of the Maunsell clearly states 'Bournemouth   ' followed by another word. This can only be 'Bournemouth West'.

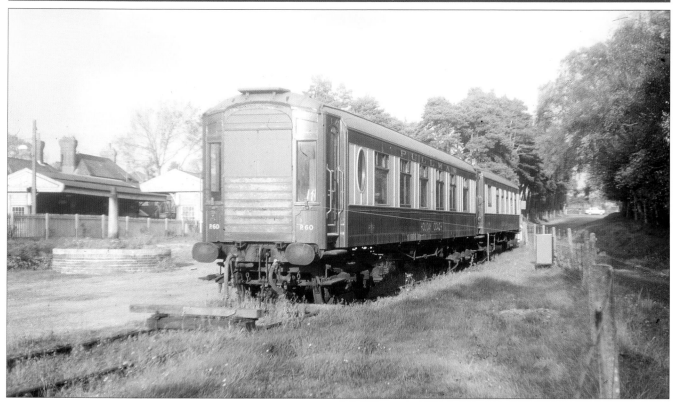

Peace and power at Sway. Above - *Deep in the heart of the New Forest at Sway two former Pullman Kitchen Cars serve out their last days as Camping Coaches. Nearest the camera is No P60, the former 'Daphne' of 1914 vintage (Birmingham Carriage & Wagon Co.) Behind is No P61, the former 'Seville' dating from 1912 and built by Messrs. Cravens. Both were withdrawn from passenger service on 9 May 1961 and sold for nearly £1,000 each to the Southern Region where, after refitting, were used as seen here at Sway until 1967. Subsequently they languished until finally broken up on site about a year later. (With thanks to Antony Ford for historical information.)* ***Below -*** *The peace is disturbed with a westbound train for Bournemouth / Weymouth.*

Above - *The mount for the slide above refers to 'No 34010, Bournemouth Central 27 October 1953'. Nice thought, anything colour from the early 1950s is most welcome except of course this cannot be correct date. The early crest would certainly support the timescale but then look behind - behold a rebuilt Bulleid. Immediately we know this now cannot be as stated, 1958 is thus more likely. It cannot be beyond this as No 34010 was rebuilt at the end of 1958.*

Opposite page - *Having seen an 'O' gauge model of a blue Merchant Navy at a show recently, there was something rather appealing about the colour scheme. I also of course regret not remembering them 'in the flesh' at that time, but pre-school was hardly the occasion to take in locomotive liveries. Here No 35018 pulls away from Southampton Central, London bound, on an unreported date. Clearly the coal did not all fit into the bunker on this particular occasion, one may indeed wonder how much actually bounced off en-route. (Were there many instances of injury or damage caused in this way?)*

Opposite top - The east side of the coaling road at Eastleigh with the office block and water tank beyond. Of the engines seen only one, No 76007 can be positively identified, and again no date is given. Pedestrian access to the depot was through a set of gates some way beyond the brick building - the usual warning notice proclaiming 'No Admittance Except on business'. It did not stop us of course, the half mile walk was nothing from the station when breaking one's journey home. Trouble is, a school satchel was a bit of a giveaway.

Opposite bottom - A 9F in Tipton yard at Eastleigh having arrived, if the first wagon is anything to go by, on Presflo cement wagons. Look carefully and a member of the footplate crew can be seen dismounting: to uncouple, or perhaps to speak to the man in the Yard Ground Frame? (We would be interested to know the working of a 9F on this type of train here. The engine is given as No 92001 and the date, 4 August 1963. In the background is the carriage works, the whole site from the platform as far as the factory itself changed beyond recognition, with rationalised track, a mountain of road-stone and modern factory units,

Above - Exmouth Junction BR Standard class 3 No 82022 at Tipton St Johns, 10 September 1960.

(All the images in this 'Colour Interlude' were purchased at shows and bear no annotation as to origin.)

Our final colour image for this issue is another from the 1950s, and shows E1R No 32124 at Exeter St Davids on 17 November 1956. The engine is probably setting off on its next banking turn from the siding known locally as the 'snake pit'.